Responsive Web Design Toolkit

Responsive Web Design Toolkit: Hammering Websites Into Shape focuses on the nuts and bolts of responsive web design, showing you how to better build and how to debug websites that use the responsive technique. This book guides you through the technology that programmers use to build, test, and debug responsive websites. Covering what engineers do, how localhost can help, and DIY-testing, this book shows technically-minded designers how to create digital objects that lead to shorter development times, quicker testing cycles, and more insight into users and their mobile devices, ultimately leading to better products.

This book:

- Gathers tools scattered across an open-sourced landscape and places them all in one, diamond-plated toolbox.
- Provides approachable, step-by-step manuals that reveal the why and how of debugging.
- Connects you with a github account where readers can find the book's source code and a companion website: www.hammeringresponsivewebdesign.com

Ken Tabor is a veteran product engineer with years of experience developing consumer-driven products on cutting-edge platforms. He shares his enthusiasm for technology as an active blogger, and frequent speaker at conferences such as SXSW Interactive, O'Reilly OSCON, and Big Design.

Ken's shipping work includes websites, mobile apps, and video games published by Atari, Nintendo, and Electronic Arts. His current emphasis is building modern solutions with open-source technology including JavaScript, HTML, Sass, Backbone, Ruby, and NodeJS. Areas of interest include mobile, UX, analytics, responsive design, leadership, chocolate, and coffee.

Over the past 4 years Ken has helped millions of travelers get where they need to go by being a leading part of the Sabre team building TripCase. TripCase is an award winning travel product comprised of a mobile website and hybrid apps for iOS and Android.

Responsive Web Design Toolkit

Hammering Websites Into Shape

By Ken Tabor

Focal Press
Taylor & Francis Group

NEW YORK AND LONDON

First published 2016
by Focal Press
70 Blanchard Road, Suite 402, Burlington, MA 01803

and by Focal Press
2 Park Square, Milton Park, Abingdon, Oxon OX14 4RN

Focal Press is an imprint of the Taylor & Francis Group, an informa business

Library of Congress Cataloging-in-Publication Data
Tabor, Ken.
    Responsive web design toolkit: hammering websites into shape / by Ken
Tabor.
        pages cm
  1. Web site development.   I. Title.
    TK5105.888.T328 2016
    006.7—dc23
    2015009835

ISBN: 978-1-138-79877-9 (pbk)
ISBN: 978-1-315-75649-3 (ebk)

Typeset in Helvetica Neue
By Apex CoVantage, LLC

Printed and bound in the United States of America by Sheridan Books, Inc. (a Sheridan Group Company).

Contents

Dedication

This book is dedicated to my daughter, Anna Tabor, who constantly reminds me that playing always leads to discovery and learning in the best possible way. Spending time with her is a tremendous joy. I'm always at my happiest when we're out in the world having adventures together.

Thanks to my parents Sharon and Dave, who supported and guided me when I was younger and continue encouraging me as I grow older. They have given me so much, and I celebrate their gifts with enthusiasm and excitement as I do my best.

Thanks to the clan in Sherman for sharing their love for life and embracing me long ago: Jan, Jim, Jessica, Ryan, Amelia, Wanda, Jeff, Karen, Jimmy, and Jennifer.

Thanks to Dave Bevans for asking me if I was interested in writing a book and guiding me through the process. Hats off to Mary LaMacchia for answering all of my never-ending questions and reassuring me when deadlines loomed. They and the good people at Focal Press took excellent care of me from start to finish, enabling me to make this happen.

Thanks to Vlad Nevzorov for kick-starting me on a journey of formal writing by focusing me on starting a technical blog. He said why not share what I've learned, because you never know where it will lead. So true!

Thanks to my supportive teammates at work: Nico, Haris, Burin, Sean, Max, Muntasir, Sanusha, Malkeet, Cindy, Tri, Natasha, Emily, Ben, Kristine, Rohit, Tomek, and Gordon.

Thanks to my friend Brian Sullivan and his constant support. I admire his leadership and drive for sustaining the local community. He's making a fantastic space for exchanging creative thoughts and opinions.

Thanks to the fantastically supportive DFW UX community and its members, who gave critiques on the book when I asked for their help, specifically Young Kim, Joe Dyer, Ben Judy, Aaron Hursman, Nathan Smith, Marti Gold, Mark Sims, and Keith Anderson.

Thanks to God and the universe for putting this fantastic opportunity in my life. As clever as I think I am, I could never have lined up all the dots that connected an unlikely path leading to writing this book.

Assembling a Toolbox of Success

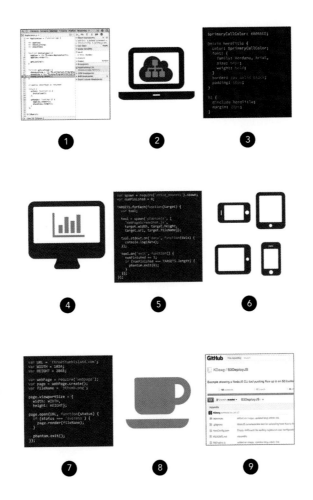

Here you'll find an overview of tools introduced in this book. Keep them in mind as you read along. You may recognize some of them but never took the time to check them out. Some probably made you think they're the exclusive domain of software engineers and out of your reach. You'll discover approachable ways of using them daily to better solve problems.

Browser Tools ❶

Modern web browsers are more than just a way to read a page. All of the popular ones have powerful tools built into them. When your website doesn't behave right, use the browser's advanced developer tools to inspect, debug, and measure what's wrong.

Web Server ❷

Running a web server on your own laptop allows you to better test your website in real-world conditions. Testing this way reveals more accurate results as you build, critique, polish, and fix your site. Finish better work before it goes out the door, when changes become more expensive.

Sass ❸

CSS is one of the big languages of the Internet. It's always up front and center, where your readers are. Writing it can be a disorganized chore, but we're all stuck with it. Craft better CSS by using a tool that translates into this language.

Analytics ❹

Building something and hoping it solves problems for your customers isn't good enough. When you add features to your website, measure how often they're used, ensuring your investment returns value for you and your visitors.

NodeJS ❺

Command-line tools are the staple of software engineers, and this JavaScript-based system allows you to build your own. Computers enjoy doing your boring tasks, allowing you time to work smarter by doing creative stuff best done by humans.

Devices ⑥

Gaining confidence that your website will work on a world of handhelds is more difficult than ever. Don't design and hope what you build will work when it goes into production. Grab phones and tablets, connect them to your laptop, and make sure your work behaves. Continually test and confirm your progress is going as expected.

PhantomJS ⑦

A web browser that doesn't display anything on screen is called headless. It's also a fantastic resource that you can experiment with. Advance your creative workflow by making interesting new tools.

Coffee ⑧

I didn't actually include coffee with this book, but I would if I could. It just seems to make a creative life better. Bring along your favorite snacks to turbo-boost your brain while studying and reading.

GitHub ⑨

The open-source community creates vast quantities of tools. Many are put on this site because it makes sharing easy. Collaboration tools are baked in, enabling creators to use and improve each other's work.

CHAPTER 1

Responsive Web Design

Why We Do It

This book won't debate whether responsive web design (RWD) is a good idea or worth our time pursuing. I can guess you've already made up your mind on that account just as I have. I consider RWD crucial for any modern web site. Given that common ground we can move forward with a goal of advancing the craft. We can put together a complete toolbox dedicated to helping you develop and, more importantly, debug your responsive web design.

I hope this book helps you when you most need an answer. Making your daily professional pursuit easier is my singular goal in writing this. Discovering a set of techniques enabling and amplifying your effort is what will happen as you travel through the pages. Reading from chapter to chapter, you'll assemble a box full of time-saving tools that build upon one another, forming a strong chain.

You will discover hands-on examples of effectively using these tools. You'll receive nuts-and-bolts examples discussing how to use them and, more significantly, when and why. Talking about problems that need solving and how to go about approaching them will empower you when replacing tools becomes necessary. Why replace tools? Some become obsolete. Some become boring, and a desire for something different drives creative inspiration.

Why should we assemble a powerful toolbox? Because debugging responsive web design isn't easy! Imagining how a page layout appears across phones, tablets, laptops, and super-wide monitors is a brain-bending exercise. Seeing how HTML, CSS, and JavaScript work across a wide selection of devices is complicated. The list of devices commonly found out in the wild isn't shrinking, either. In fact it's expanding as Android devices grow and exotic machines appear. You may already be targeting glasses, watches, and thermostats.

This book will share immediately useful concepts, helping you more safely navigate one of the most difficult things we tackle: building websites that respond to a world of devices.

When you get to a point that it feels as though you wish you could throttle a website into submission by hammering it into shape, I expect tools and techniques found in this book will give you the confidence and strength to debug your designs into working order.

An audience of technically minded designers will find practical topics in this book such as:

- Delay expensive hardware purchases as long as possible by emulating devices in your development environment.

- Turn around work iterations more quickly by setting up a web server on your Windows and OS X machine.

- Write more readable and maintainable CSS by using Sass.

- Explore the power of NodeJS and PhantomJS to generate multisized portfolios.

As we review each of these concepts, reason is always applied: reasons we reach for a particular tool, how to wield it, and the creative power it's meant to amplify. While technology changes and tools are replaced, the reason to use them remains.

MOTION FASCINATION

Here's an admission: When I discover a website that's built responsively, I'll play with it, seeing how it reacts. I love playing. It's such a fantastic way to learn. My daughter taught me how to wonder through play without expectation. She's always curious, open minded, and ready to see.

I try taking on that point of view as I pull my web browser frame from right to left, slowly making it smaller. Small enough until it's the width of a phone. Then with a pause of admiration, I'll drag the browser's right edge back to full screen's width, watching how it responds to my movement. How does it fill a desktop screen size?

The act of screen layout destruction and creation fascinates me. What pieces decide to shrink down? What sections pop away? What springs into life, hidden until my movements reveal them? How does the site decide to break down anticipating the viewer's screen width? Responsive design is a brief, choreographed dance performed for my audience of one.

Do you do the same thing? Admire the complicated beauty that unfurls as a sail blowing full in the wind before collapsing down into stillness? Orchestrating that composition is not without heartache. It demands dedication. Making it look smooth and effortless takes tremendous effort. Dynamic, user-driven interaction remains one of the most compelling aspects of our digital world. It's the reason for responsive web development.

Inspiring the content in this book is a desire to serve technically minded designers and web developers. Anyone wanting to power up their craft of delivering their responsive websites more quickly will find serious tools here.

RESPONSIVE WEB DESIGN: A BRIEF
HISTORY AND EXPLANATION

If we asked a group of people to define responsive web design, what answers would you expect to hear? More than likely, we'd get descriptions. People would tell us qualities of what it is and what it isn't. Perhaps we'd hear about popular libraries and frameworks used for successfully building responsive designs. Fluidity, adaptivity, grid-based formats, media queries, and breakpoints might be mentioned.

You and I probably share similar expectations for responsive web design. They're relatively simple given the overall complex topic. For each category of device (phone, tablet, laptop), the site best fits to the capacity of the viewer's hardware. It's amazing that all possible views are held within a unified design architecture, showing enough information, enabling our customers to effectively interact with our technology.

Observations on implementation details are honest reflections of our current understanding. It's informed by engaging in development, consuming responsive sites, and being interested in the community's best practices.

A few years back, facing the increasingly diverse array of screen sizes our customers view our websites with, our industry had to invent a technique, one promising that our sites look and work well for all. Responsive web design was, and for the most part currently is, the primary solution for that complicated challenge.

Desiring a richer context on the domain, I discovered Ethan Marcotte's May 2010 article on A List Apart to be one of the earliest opinions on the matter. In his article, Marcotte compares the relatively transient nature of software and websites to the relative permanence of architecture. More significantly, he teases out metaphors drawing upon a building's foundation, footprint, and potential for flexibility.

There surely is a losing battle in a pursuit of making designs specifically for a given form factor. So many screen resolutions exist that keeping up is traveling a maddening path with only loss of time and sanity found at the end.

We can easily agree with a client's request for supporting typical screen sizes: "oh yes phone, tablet, laptop." In that very assurance, we know phones come in 4- and 5-inch versions. We know tablets come in 7- and 10-inch forms. We know computers have all sorts of dimensions as well as external monitors. Further still, my videogame station hooked up to my living room HDTV has a high-end web browser.

Marcotte spells out the underpinning concept so well.

> We can design for an optimal viewing experience, but embed standards-based technologies into our designs to make them not only more flexible, but more adaptive to the media that renders them. In short, we need to practice responsive web design.
> "Responsive Web Design," last modified May 25, 2010,
> http://alistapart.com/article/responsive-web-design

Seek out that article when you have the time if you've not read it. Even more fun for me is that Marcotte's proof-of-concept web pages remain functional. They demonstrate his techniques, which are relevant today.

As a product engineer, I admire his initiative looking at real-world references, such as buildings and architecture for inspiration and convention that our digital world might use. Often enough, I'm stuck on a horridly demanding problem, and success comes into view as I look at the problem through the lens of other industries.

ADJUSTING FOR ALL SHAPES AND SIZES

How many screen sizes are there? What's a realistic count that we need to support? Is it actually so complicated? Yes, certainly more than we know.

Treating a new user or perspective customer to a sad experience is the worst. Anything less than a great experience lets your audience drift away to your competitor. The viewer doesn't have an investment hooking them into figuring out your site.

As a study, I've reviewed my blog analytics. I found that approximately 350 different screen sizes have shown up while users are reading my articles. Of course I need to serve each and every one of them, or I feel that I've failed. Fortunately I've built my blog with responsive web design in mind. RWD allows me to satisfy my readers by fitting my content into their screens in the best way possible.

Reading that statistic, someone might exclaim "Three hundred and fifty! How can that many screen sizes exist? Sure, we have many phones, several tablets, lots of computers, and a couple of external monitors, but that's not possible." A fair reaction.

Not only mobile devices figure into the count. In fact every time someone resizes their web browser on a computer they're hitting my blog with a different view. Their experience is uniquely theirs, and if my blog carried ten times the readership traffic, I'm sure I'd see at least double or triple the number of screen sizes.

Looking at the analytics data, I see visitors presenting groups of screen sizes.

Amount of Visitors	Amount of Screen Sizes
62%	Top five
87%	Top ten
93%	Top fifteen

Trailing behind the top fifteen is a long tail of random shapes and sizes, probably representing whatever resolution my readers resized their desktop browser to before navigating to my site. Don't be too worried, because order does emerge from this randomness. Easily recognized sizes typical of phones, tablets, and laptops are counted among the top fifteen most popular visitors to my blog. Similar patterns will show on your site as well.

If you're looking at that screen size data and thinking its insights are totally useful, I agree. We can turn data into knowledge, understanding what our customers need from us. If you're thinking I must have labored getting the data in the chart above, that's the awesome part. Getting those numbers is simple. Because reporting them only takes five minutes, I refer to them often.

EMPATHY FOR OUR USERS

Anyone in charge of project budgets thinking responsive web design is a magical solution because "we build it once and it works on anything, all the platforms come for free, and it's cheaper because we build the UI once instead of three times" misunderstands the technique. It's more expensive and more difficult than creating a user interface (UI) for a single device. It takes more brain-sweat, more paper prototyping, more mindful consideration of everything your user wants to do on your site. Enabling them to consume your content with devices of any size can feel mind blowing, but we'll make it easier starting today.

Early on, if we can imagine how our users connect with our website, we can encourage that connection. Ensuring it's as straight a line as possible without distracting turns down broken paths is compassionate as well as valuable.

Debugging and Testing Versus Writing Responsive Web Design

Every page of this book supports your goal of crafting a fantastic user experience founded on responsive design principles. Please understand that very little time is spent in the design or implementation of RWD simply because dozens of books and hundreds of blog articles already cover that.

Someone might ask, "Is writing the files making up a responsive website easy?" and I'd answer, "No way." We do know that many books and articles exist to serve that audience. In fact, every website on the Internet is a functional example showing CSS, HTML, and JavaScript. All that's needed is a web browser with solid inspection tools.

Given that, I turn your attention to the next steps in the creative workflow:

- Testing and debugging
- Rapid iteration in your developer environment
- Emulating production servers locally
- Simulating user device screen sizes

Where will these next-level tools come from? In many ways, it's mindfully adapting parts of the tool chain that at first appear to be the exclusive domain of software engineers. Pulling over parts of their toolbox means strengthening the toolset of technically minded designers and developers. The goal is clearly demonstrating in practical ways that you can easily understand, appreciate, and leverage, all in service of making you more productive and elevating you above your peers.

Testing and debugging is a constant focus throughout this book. It's not good enough to only write all the files making up a website, because at some point, they must be run on user devices. Before they are, we'd better confirm the site operates with an acceptable level of quality. Detecting problems, reproducing them, discovering what causes them, and turning around changes is an ongoing process. Using powerful code-inspection tools makes finding bugs easier.

Rapid iteration makes bug finding and fixing more joyful. Discovering a problem with our work makes us sad pandas, but fixing them quickly brings happiness. How do we shorten that loop? How do we stay in the creative flow more often? One way is bringing live production environments, such as web servers, onto the same computers where we create our work.

Emulating production servers helps us find and fix bugs. If we can create, test, debug, and verify code and art changes on our own computers, development time decreases and happiness increases. Comfort and convenience go a long way. Being on our own machines leads to that. Installing the same web server used in live production on our computer enables us to see our work nearly the same way our users will. We can see our website as they do, identify as them, and meet their needs before they arrive.

Simulating user device screen sizes, again on our work computer, is a fine way to test our design seeing it as our users will. Identifying as them, practically by way of their viewing machines, allows us helpful insight into our creation.

Making all of the tasks easily done, repeatable, means we reality check often. Reducing friction of a process means people will do it more often. In this case, it's a very good thing indeed. This relates to automation.

Automation is highly valued. The thinking is that as the complexity to do a thing is lowered to a point that it's free to do, why wouldn't an individual or team do more of that? Especially when it delivers a better user experience. We will review automation in some chapters because it's a competitive advantage.

RESOURCES FOR RESPONSIVE WEB DESIGN

Many excellent sources explaining the design process, from sketching through paper prototyping to authoring source code, are out there. Where their voices grow silent is on the grueling task of developers testing and debugging against an ever-growing array of devices.

This book focuses on filling the gap between writing code and a site appearing on users' devices. Much time is spent assisting you in more easily testing your design, more rapidly turning around source code changes, and more soundly debugging it. Ways of incorporating reality checks such as simulating production server environments and screen sizes without hardware are crucial topics.

Designers, artists, and developers wanting more guidance on designing and planning ought to look for alternatives. Typical RWD implementation topics like the following are not covered here:

- Grid-based frameworks
- CSS and HTML boilerplates

- Media queries and breakpoints
- Wireframe strategies

All of these topics are crucial for our craft, and I want every reader of this book to succeed at them. Learn more about them by spending time in the search engine of your choice plugging in those keywords.

Once you've internalized those concepts and are building a website, please crack open this book for concrete ways of reviewing and validating your designs. You'll find that troublesome effort can be done more easily, cheaply, and generally more happily.

THIS BOOK IS FOR YOU IF YOU'RE SEEKING EASIER DEVELOPMENT

In my opinion, "development" incorporates the entire process of building software rather than any particular job. Everyone who has a concrete touchpoint in an application or website is a "developer." Why does that matter? It's to assure readers of this book that it's not written with programmers in mind. In fact, many of us feel that artists are evolving into roles that pull tasks for writing code as well as traditional look, layout, and workflow. In my mind, this is a technically minded designer. It's high time to raise them up.

Designers are the primary audience for this book, but everyone on the team will take away something useful for making their job easier. Benefits abound for teammates who gleefully cross boundaries but take a deep dive in some specialty skill. Let's get out from behind our silos and see what other folks are doing!

Working closely together comes naturally for generalists at start-ups. Everyone must seemingly do everything just to willfully pull it off the ground. Furthermore, cross-functional teams are found in any number of companies.

What are key challenges for developing responsive design?

- A single page of content is seen with multiple looks.
- There is no single definition for what a phone and tablet screen size is.
- Developer computers are not configured to match customer-facing environments.
- Writing CSS becomes complicated as more media queries are built into styles.

If responsive web development is as complicated as all this, who would ever want to do it? In fact, we know who demands it: our customers, made up of end users and clients paying for modern websites.

What are specific ways this book makes responsive web development easier?

- Strengthening your development workflow
- Increasing your tooling options
- Providing multiple ways to look at the page content
- Simulating device specific resolutions

- Matching up authoring and production environments
- Iterating the classic design–code–test–fix lifecycle rapidly

HELPING DESIGNERS AND MORE

Anyone building modern-day websites will benefit from the lessons contained in this book. It's not just designers but also technically minded artists, web developers, quality-assurance testers, and leaders managing creative teams.

Technically minded designers will gain insights into the next level of development, incorporating ways of testing websites by emulating how users view their work. Installing servers that closely match final live production environments helps diagnose glitches earlier in the build process, when changes are less costly.

Quality-assurance experts may want to incorporate ways of emulating devices on their own computers with an eye toward delaying expensive hardware orders for as long as possible. Analytics reporting reveals what mobile devices are used the most and are therefore most worth budget spending.

Leaders will take away concrete strategies for reducing time to market and development expenses. Techniques show ways of directing their teams of designers and developers to fail fast. The goal is seeking out problems and glitches before they hit customer-facing environments.

Developers straight-up coding websites will have a new sense of joy when incorporating these tools. The drudgery of making wireframes and design mockups functional by coding them up will be easier as verification techniques are introduced.

How Does This Book Work?

THE BOOK'S STRUCTURE

Chapters are grouped to introduce you to new tools, explain their use, and then progressively advance your knowledge through new applications of them. Each chapter flows together from end to beginning, but you'll see a few major groupings.

Chapters 1 and 2 contain an introduction to the book's mission and the concept of adapting engineering tools and process to your daily workflow.

Chapters 3 through 6 introduce you to the importance of web servers and walk you through the steps necessary for installing, setting up, and using one on your own work machine.

Chapters 7 through 10 each survey a particular tool that will help you raise your expertise in web development, making responsive web development easier.

Chapters 11 and 12 conclude the book with a special project connecting the dots between several open-source tools, creating a highly customized megatool!

TIP BOXES

You'll find boxes throughout the chapters pulled away from the regular text. These are totally optional reading, but they are linked to the lessons around them. Each offers additional details explaining some concept introduced in that section. Because they're deep dives into the related subjects, feel to read them at your leisure or even skip them for a while.

COMPANION WEBSITE

I've made a website to accompany this book. Give it a look from time to time to see what's new. I'll be sharing on it the latest info I find on new tools that will help you hammer RWD into shape. I'll also write answers in response to whatever questions I receive from you and your fellow book readers.

```
http://HammeringResponsiveWebDesign.com
```

Assembling a Toolbox of Success

Anyone can walk over to the neighborhood hardware store to buy a hammer and screwdriver. It's one thing to have the tools stacked on a work surface in the garage, but it's another to know when to use them for solving a recognized problem.

It's another talent to know when a tool needs to be replaced. Technology changes all the time. Hammers look very much the same as they did a hundred years ago. Software tools are a trickier matter. Compare two that solve the same problem, and they might install, behave, and act differently. Understanding the job you're trying to finish directly influences what tool you reach for today. It also reveals the capabilities you seek out in its replacement tomorrow.

Ultimately, by following along with this book, you'll assemble a compete toolbox of modern power tools specifically arranged for your success. Ideally, you'll meet deadlines more quickly, leapfrog your peers, suffer less frustration, and stay more deeply immersed in the creative flow. You might even be happier!

CHAPTER 2

Introducing the Engineering Process

What Do Engineers Do?

I grew up using tools. You did too. I still recall going through my grandfather's basement workshop looking at his lifelong collection of tools and wondering if I'd ever have as many as he did. He was an electrician and master of his craft. He had tiny jeweler-quality screwdrivers and iron pipe benders as tall as I was, plus electric drills, power saws, and sledgehammers. He was always encouraging, but I can see now that he only taught me about tools I asked about when he thought I was ready to handle them with respect. These were amazing things for me to learn when I was young. They activated my thirst for discovering, learning careful use. My attitude wasn't always sensible and respectful, I admit. I burned, shocked, cut, and scared myself plenty, but I always learned—often what not to do as much as how to properly do things. Some of my grandfather's tools are in my personal collection, and when I reach for them, his patient lessons inform my decisions.

My grandfather had all kinds of tools, but most of them were dedicated to a single purpose. Each was built to solve a particular problem well, but only that one. Computers fascinate me because they're the ultimate tool. Software adapts them to solve interesting problems for all types of people with all sorts of jobs. By writing a new program, I can make the computer solve new problems for different audiences: word processing, artistic painting, music composition, accounting spreadsheets, magazine layout, adrenaline-junkie driving. While solving problems for people, computers often democratized those people's jobs. Suddenly we didn't need a person to do a thing for us; we could load software that helps us do that job. Creative freedom to do a task is a wonderful thing, but it does make me appreciate that inborn talent and years of skill are worth paying experts for.

Growing up as a kid, I was lucky because my stepdad worked for IBM. He bought one of their first personal computers off the assembly line through employee purchase. I cannot imagine he knew what a home computer would do to me, but it captured my imagination totally and completely. Learning programming languages and making software utterly defined my career. In fact, it entirely defined my lifelong interests and unlocked my potential.

WHAT DO ENGINEERS KNOW?

What's the point of this chapter? Software engineers and programmers know stuff that's important to them, and that's fine, but what does that matter to artists, designers, and developers? A lot, as a matter of fact. The job of artists and designers is getting more technical every year. Any of them building websites by writing HTML, CSS, and even JavaScript are in fact programming. Using jQuery and pulling down plugins is integrating libraries just as engineers would. Stylesheet languages, like LESS and Sass are compiled just like the languages that programmers classically use. Because these powerful tools are easily available for free from publically accessed websites, they're democratizing the job of software engineers.

Let's continue embracing that skillful movement and mix in more, not to a point of complexity but to connect more dots drawing a line toward new, disciplined goals. I say that professional discipline is what separates hackers and rookies from veteran masters of their craft. We ought to mindfully explore what tools we can bring into our creative workflow, turbo-boosting it to the next level. What are the nuts-and-bolts technologies and techniques that better enable us to deliver quality work, help our teammates, and lend assistance to our community?

It's my opinion as a software engineer that my community has access to a deep set of tools and techniques that help us better perform our web development work.

Traditionally, that toolset stays within our culture simply for the lack of trying to share it in a simple way with other fields. I don't want that to continue happening. Tools are an important part of our job, but so too is the understanding of how we choose them, how we apply them, and how we decide to improve or replace them.

Technology is constantly on the move around us. Principles forming our professional foundation stay the same. As programming languages and platforms are replaced, our desire to master craft and point of view on what we want from our tools persists. You'll see the meaning and value behind those attitudes conveyed in this chapter.

POWERFUL TOOLS FOR A STRONG CRAFT

Tooling is absolutely crucial to developing software. Always has been and always will be. Make no mistake that websites are software. They capture lists of rules telling computers how to behave. In this case, the behavior drives a web browser, telling it how to reach for assets and display those for a user, and waits for that viewer to interact with it. If someone tries to discount your accomplishments by saying it's only HTML, CSS, JavaScript, and images, I'll tell them it's without a doubt a computer program.

In my opinion, building software at scale is the second most complicated thing human beings do. Computers execute rules flawlessly, without hesitation, time and again. Therefore the software logic governing their actions must be flawless. Are human authors capable of flawless work? In other words, can they obtain perfection? Absolutely not, but we think we can. Tools can help.

Tools reduce the complexity of creating perfect websites. One of the ways they do this is by validating our syntax—the words and symbols we type to make our program. In other words, they double-check how we use the grammar of the computer world.

We need help staying more deeply in the creative workflow. Tools watching our work and calling out problems help do that. Bugs and defects in our flawed logic are found more quickly, certainly before problems escape our work computers and get out into the public, where they are more costly—and possibly more embarrassing—to fix.

In real life, the tools you've grown up using on projects around the house are easily recognized as time-saving power-ups. You come to quickly understand the use of a hammer, rope, and screwdriver and quickly reach for one when the need arises. You can conveniently buy these at your corner hardware store. Software tools amplify your strengths and abilities in the same way, but finding the right ones is a more difficult problem. Sometimes a front-end development tool goes out of style soon after you hear of it. Often you don't even know what the choices are.

Choosing your tools at the start of a project is a uniquely personal and important task. Don't do it quickly just to check a box for your company's chief technology officer (CTO) or art director. Because you're a knowledge worker, your software tools are an extension of your creative workflow, imagination, and even identity. Tools influence the way you work and affect who will join you in your work. Remember that you have a choice and that your choice matters, and please make good choices.

OPTIMIZE FOR CHANGE

Reflecting on my career, I've decided there's only one constant, and that's change. Engineers writing computer program eventually get to the point of talking about optimizing their work. It's where they invest their greatest effort, concentrated brain sweat, to purposefully write their code, sometimes rewriting the code multiple times until the desired results is achieved. I've observed a few common patterns for how software engineers optimize their programs:

- Attaining the fastest running performance
- Consuming the least amount of memory possible
- Using every feature available in the language
- Expressing their own personal style
- Attaining the quickest build time

One or more of these may be important for your project, but in my opinion we ought to focus on optimizing for change. Your time is always limited. In my 25-year career, I've used eight major operating systems and written in 13 programming languages while building websites, games, apps, and tools. Given all of the changes I've seen, I have no doubt I'm going to see even more, and I expect you will, too.

Consider how your projects change over time. It happens constantly, and we might as well accept that and work within that constraint. Giving up the illusion that we know what the market, users, owners, and clients will want is liberating. After admitting we won't, don't, and can't know enough to properly plan, we can finally build code in the most flexible way possible. We can incorporate as many tools as we can possibly find to help us build an ever-evolving website, experience, and code base. Creative work such as ours means lots of experimentation. We're never quite sure if what we think in our heads will be good enough when our customers get their hands on it through their devices. Creative leaders should set up a culture in which work can start before all the requirements are discovered, because they never will be. Being comfortable and productive in uncertainty is a highly desirable skill in modern teammates.

Allow for flexibility from the start when defining your testing strategy and development workflow. Design your websites and apps in ways that make it easy to change appearance, function, and deployment. Provide for changes based on advice given by customer feedback. Remind your teammates of this goal and work together on keeping your agility as high as possible.

SOURCE CODE

Source code sounds very serious and like it's something only engineers create. Of course that's a ridiculous assumption. Every website is based on source code. If you're building a website and write HTML, CSS, and JavaScript, then you're producing source code. Source code is one of the most valuable assets a company possesses. (Perhaps the most important one is a fully engaged team living in a vibrant, creative, collaborative culture.)

Because source code is crucial to what we do as professionals, we must guard it well. It's an asset to our clients and company, and once we're done making a website, the code behind it is precious. In fact, it's precious while we're making it and ought to be treated as a rare treasure. Programmers use a tool called source control that helps maintain source code in a protected way. Source control is a program that keeps source code on a server, offering precise ways of reading and writing to it. That makes it easier for a team to share parts of a program with one another in an organized way. Changes are made in order, kept separately, and recorded in order by date and time. This is called revision history. Programmers like history because it organizes changes submitted by different people on the same files. Everyone must line up in an orderly fashion as the source control system orchestrates updates. If a change unexpectedly turns out badly, the team can refer to the revision history and pull out broken changes, exchanging them for working ones. It's a massive help.

Source control systems are a specific topic worthy of your time, but this book will not take the time to dive deeply into them. You'll see some reference to them in Chapter 7 as it reviews how to use projects from one of the more popular and public systems called GitHub. When you want to learn more about source control tools, please look up information on these types of systems: SVN, Git, CVS, and Mercurial.

SINGLE CODE BASE

Maintaining source code can seem like a full-time job for a creative leader as a team and project gain in size. One reason I admire responsive development is that it tries keeping all views of a website within the same project. There's no need for two projects representing a desktop site and a mobile site. Over the past years, a dedicated mobile site was a way of solving the complexity of building for handhelds while also supporting laptop and desktop users. This has become a problem because it means two completely separate projects, each with its own source code and probably its own dedicated team. Organizational problems are rife in this environment, and now that solution feels like an example of what not to do. It's become an antipattern and a cautionary tale.

Responsive development allows a creative team leader to combine previously separated desktop and mobile teams to work together on the same base of source code. They can pair up, solving problems together. Delivering a shared effort lets people get smarter about the project. Now the designers and developers have richer context for the entire project. They can cover each other through illness and vacations and generally empathize with one another, strengthening team bonds while shipping working websites together. Tools become more important to test this shared work because it must be more flexible, considering the world of device sizes we must embrace.

LAZY PROGRAMMERS ARE HAPPIER

Business drives us to be more productive, innovative, and engaged. Does it make sense to admit we're lazy workers or that we aspire to laziness? I'll shout yes every time I have the chance. When I say "lazy," does that mean I don't want to work as hard as someone else? That I'm a cynical burnout whose best years are behind him? Not in the least! I'm driven to perfect and master my craft more than ever.

What I don't want to do is pull a task, open my text editor, and start blasting code. It's wrong to assume I know the solution to a problem from the very start. I'd rather invest some time early on discovering what a task is and why it exists. Can I break down a story feature into smaller tasks? Then discover what pieces someone else has already figured out and published as libraries, plugins, or recipes that I can pull into my project? If I can spend 1 hour avoiding 6 hours of work, then I'm winning.

Where does this code come from? The open sources community is distributed in different ways:

- Packaged libraries downloadable from official websites
- Source code repositories hosted on collaborative coding sites such as GitHub and SourceForge

- Snippets written in live coding sites like CodePen and PasteBin

- Solutions on discussion sites like StackOverflow

- Embedded in detailed popular technical blogs

External sites like those are relatively easily found with enough questions typed into your favorite web search engine. More fun for me is discovering ones that are inside my company. They are more difficult to find, perhaps, because it usually means being at your company long enough and knowing people there who have seen such libraries built over time. Some are already inside your project's source code, but others are hosted in potentially weird spots that only old-timers know.

Building libraries for yourself, your team, and your company is crucial. Answers discovered and solutions made are investments in your future. Creative leaders, please encourage your team to think in these terms. Sometimes a problem is so difficult that your team is relieved when it's over and moves along. Take time to celebrate the solution, teach others about it, and build a plugin or library or write a page on your wiki. Demand your team makes new bugs. Mistakes are opportunities to learn, and we only fail when we don't learn the lessons and make them again.

Code reuse is an ideal state. Libraries, modules, and plugins are little nuggets of hard-earned knowledge that make life easier. Try building each of those in a way that it solves one particular problem in an excellent way. Resist the temptation of improving them to a point where people are confused why the library exists. Please consider building solutions to future problems from current learning.

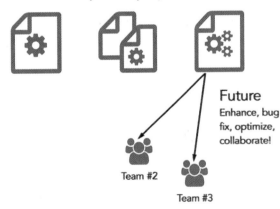

Lazy Programmers Prosper

Write code once, copy it again, but after that make a reusable library, replace the others, and share it

1st Time
Blast out some code and make it work well.

2nd Time
Copy and paste just to get the job done quickly.

3rd Time
Create reusable library, replace 1st and 2nd.

Team #2

Team #3

Future
Enhance, bug fix, optimize, collaborate!

When you come to the point of building something like this, consider ways to share. Certainly share with your own team, but think of the company if it's a modest-sized agency or a large enterprise. If there's a chance, find out if you can add your reusable component to the open-source community. It's a great way to share and attract goodwill, new teammates, and additional help with your work. Open-source projects benefit from crowd-sourced solutions. Imagine people volunteering to improve your work with new features, optimizations, bug fixes, and unit tests.

Every programming language has a community that you can be a part of, whether it's server-side technologies like NodeJS and Ruby or client-side languages like HTML and CSS.

Share

How can a soft skill like sharing possibly matter to a creative leader aiming to arrange a high-performing team? It seems too easy an answer. Let me assure you that emphasizing a culture of sharing is one of the single most powerful things that you can do. "Share," in the true sense of the word, encompasses a complex and subtle combination of values.

Sharing Virtuous Cycle

When novel creativity delivers value

? Curiosity

🚀 Delivery   **⚡** Discovery

👥 Teaching   **⚙** Invention

Learn something to share. You'll always work hard on the job, but realize that genuine learning happens off the clock. Read blogs, follow your favorite creators, trace through open-source code, build side projects on your own time. Why? Because personal hobby projects are where the real learning happens, as you're creative only for creativity's sake. It's the artist's territory where chasing down fantastic paths of true invention is the only thing that matters. There's no customer past yourself, no deadline past your own hours, and no goal but solving interesting problems.

As your passion projects spring from daydreaming and into reality, take a chance to demo your experiments to your team. Invest in them, offering a tour of all the work you've done. How will they respond? Perhaps they'll take it and build on your ideas in surprising ways. Bringing something useful and valuable to your team will make everyone around you better.

Listen when someone is sharing. Does your team respect one another enough to stop what they're doing, turn full attention to the speaker, and invest their time in hearing what they say? One of the meetings I run at my job is a purposeful forum for sharing code and pro tips. My only rule to the gathered audience is giving the speaker complete attention. It's proper at a professional level and validating at a basic human level. Deep learning comes from hearing, and that comes from deliberately listening.

Cross-train when someone is sharing. Meeting to discuss the most recently solved problems gives the team a chance to celebrate the little successes as they grind out tasks and hit deadlines. Recognizing a job well done is fuel for creative minds to power past the difficulties projects inevitably present. Hard-earned knowledge ought to be spread out among the team. Any answer to a bug fix or CSS workaround is an investment, and passing it around a team lets you grow earnings from the time spent. Spreading answers among people helps break down silos for common understanding and covers the day when the original inventor isn't around. That happens all the time. Could be that they quit the company, transferred to another group, or were on vacation.

Team build when someone is sharing. Cultural memes are like a viral infection spreading among the brains in your team. Let them demonstrate to one another what's expected while sharing. New hires will quickly realize that you have a team of outstanding players who seek out others possessing curious minds. Sharing is a sure way to foster candid revelations that leads to solid collaboration. When someone encounters a problem similar to what their teammate encountered, they know what tool or technique to reach for. Remind one another to make each other better by sharing what's discovered.

Creative leaders know their purpose is enabling their teams. Enabling them to do what? Someone might say to do better work more often. I think it's to help a group of individuals realize how to perform well together.

Rothman and Derby paint a vivid description of how my favorite teams have worked well together.

> If you've ever worked on a jelled team, you know how good it feels. A jelled team has energy. People accomplish great feats. They celebrate and laugh together. They disagree and argue but not disagreeably. Jelled teams don't happen by accident; teams jell when someone pays attention to building trust and commitment. The jelled teams we've seen create and work towards shared goals. Over time they build trust by exchanging and honoring commitments to each other.
>
> Johanna Rothman and Esther Derby, *Behind Closed Doors: Secrets of Great Management* (USA: The Pragmatic Programmers, 2008, p. 49)

GAINING CONFIDENCE

You may know engineers as an argumentative bunch. We hold many opinions on a wide variety of topics and are happy to voice our positions. Although it seems we're extremely confident in our firmly held beliefs, I can't help but think we're always searching for confidence. We know that computers will flawlessly follow our instructions without hesitation or deviation. As we write instructions in the form of programs, we know that we human authors are teeming with flaws and uncertainty. It's the nature of our limited ability to predict the future. In fact, while computers are flawless at running programs, we know they're flawed, and we know the people using them are just as flawed. Users can't follow directions and make mistakes while they believe they're following them correctly. If we can't write programs well and expect our customers to make mistakes while using them, what hope is there for success?

Gaining confidence through testing is one way programmers know when they can reliably ship code. Testing techniques and tools are found throughout this book. The goal is finding ways to test on our working computers as often as possible. Staying deeply entranced in the creative zone is key to improving productivity while making the most of our always-limited time. While we want to pinpoint bugs, glitches, and edge-cases on our own work computers, it's important to realize the true fact: Unless we test our code on real mobile hardware, it doesn't matter in the least how much work we've done. Strategies for testing on hardware are addressed in this book.

Testing by hand is referred to as manual testing. Another tactic is automated testing using various software that emulates human interactions with your software. That won't be covered in this book, but plenty of material exists on this subject.

Fear of failure is something that we all have. It's instinctive, and no matter how experienced we are, it's worth keeping humble while building software. Nothing yet has moved me from my opinion that building software at scale is the second-hardest thing human beings do. Testing lets us move quickly with confidence. It's important to continue polishing, improving, and evolving our website's abilities and user experience. Testing helps keep that process moving forward.

BUILD. MEASURE. LEARN.

When we build something, how do we know it's used? Do we wait for user reviews? Do we wait for confused support emails? How can we decide our investment in building a feature was worth the return? Sometimes it's easier than others. For example, some features will obviously deliver immediate business value in terms of revenue. We might have secondary benefits that don't provide money but offer other value, such as engagement or acquisition. For these types of features, you ought to implement analytics.

By default, most analytics record when a user hits a web page, which is useful, for example, when you're building a blog formed from a collection of articles. What about measuring customer interaction on a page with settings, buttons, and sliders? What about a complex web page that's more like an application than a document? Properly engineering analytics can measure when users tap and slide on a page. Unique interactions can be tracked as interaction events. Sometimes it's enough to say how often a UI element is used on a page. Sometimes you want to establish a funnel where all the people in the universe can start, some drop off, but others continue along the workflow, step by step, until a smaller group finishes. Analytics provide the factual measure of those steps.

Facts allow us to cut through opinions, gut instinct, and tradition and decide with evidence of our customers' use of our website and web apps. Watch arguments fall away as your team reviews the analytics reporting dashboard and sees exactly how often specific pages are viewed and particular UI widgets are used. Numbers don't lie, and analytics disclose candid insights. Find out if an investment has paid off by implementing some form of analytics in your development process and business practice. If it becomes a part of your culture, you'll find it a material advantage over the competition.

Don't fire and forget, either. Once you build something, follow up each day, week, month, or quarter and report its use. Craft a dashboard that specifically reports performance on mobile devices (desktop, too, when it's relevant). Some feature that's not accomplishing what you expect needs an investment. Schedule time to improve it, or remove it. There are no failures as long as we learn from past performance and choose a different future path.

Anaytics Reporting

Measure the user experience as users are experiencing it

	1st	2nd	3rd	4th
iOS Version	8.1	8.0.2	7.1.1	6.0
Resolution	375x667	320x568	320x480	360x640
Bounce Rate	72%	77%	76%	81%
Device Brand	Apple	Samsung	Google	LG
Event Tracking	File/Open	Search/Game	Map/Open	Contact/Add

When you build something, measure it and learn from its results. Bring analytics into your creative tool chain as soon as possible. Let facts guide your decisions. Any large-scale organization might be adding a new job called business intelligence. Don't let the khaki-and-blue-shirt–wearing pointy-hairs in biz-dev become gatekeepers of the analytics reports. Go get the data, dig deeply into it, and own the results. I encourage you to have heart when you see all the numbers behind analytics. Default dashboards can appear as big-data overload and disable an entire segment of your team. Tell them how important it is to get behind these numbers and not the math that computes them. Craft custom reporting dashboards, and the graphed data will look like art. The numbers will measure your users' experiences while they actively use the experience.

WE'RE ALL MAKERS TOGETHER

Building software can be a solo pursuit, but at its finest, there are teams of skilled individuals working together. Creative leaders are always trying to get their teams of people working better together. They want to organize their groups to work with purpose and toward a common objective. Ensuring everyone on the team has a shared understanding of what the work is marks the first step of that journey. Listening to stakeholder requirements and building user personas and story-based workflows are all useful tools in coming to a shared understanding. In my mind, past all that, it's a people problem, and figuring out how to build the team's capacity to deliver together becomes the crucial goal.

Much is published about finding individuals who are rock stars, front-end unicorns, or full-stack developers. This wrongly celebrates the ability of a single person rather than the capacity of a team. When the team is fully integrated, with personnel filling all needed skills, then you're building capacity to deliver excellent work. Once the team fully gels to a point that they act almost with a single-minded attitude, then the company will deliver the best work possible in the shortest amount of time.

Building full-stack teams delivering together will involve finding front-end programmers, testers, designers, and product owners. Whenever possible, ensure they sit together. Let them overhear each other's conversations so that someone with the answer might easily share it. Break down silos if they exist. It's an antipattern to have all the company's designers, programmers, testers, and product owners sitting separated by job title. Teams can do better when each individual understands a little about everyone else's job, too. Your team should be full stack, having all the talent to deliver any feature. When employees of a particular skill or job are exclusively sitting together, then their daily exposure lacks diversity. They lose sight of what other teammates do in their jobs.

Silos might be a problem for your team if programmers "throw their code over the wall" to testers for them to find the bugs. If the answer to a question about a possible bug is "it works on my machine," then your team is dysfunctional and producing below capacity. Encourage your programmers to give a quick demo to testers and even to product owners and designers before putting a task in the "ready for test" column. Even a 5-minute demo reveals small glitches needing more work. Use this as a chance for the team to expose assumptions, discuss edge-cases, and catch up with last-minute decisions together. Put a little more work into it before it goes to test, and certainly before it goes to your end customers.

Silos might be a problem for your team if product owners are delivering documents to designers before the testing and programming team hears about it. Encourage your product owners to deliver a brief pitch to the collected team. Reveal why the team ought to build or change something. What is the business case and why is it valuable? In meetings like this, you'll find that testers are fantastic at thinking like real customers. Let them break down assumptions and discover gaps in workflows. It's time to crowd source answers together. Programmers can offer observations about the feature requests given the context of the website they've already built. Let them make suggestions to maintain consistency across the site. Designers have an early opportunity to offer up best practices in user experience and new UI mechanics. It's a chance to talk together, and that breaks down walls and builds up trust.

Silos might be a problem for your team if your designers get a feature request from a product owner and then go dark for days, building a series of pixel-perfect mockups that are dropped off to developers to build as shown. This waterfall approach to development misses the opportunity for a rich discussion among programmers, designers, testers, and product owners. With communication, there's a chance to establish shared understanding early and maintain it throughout a feature and project. Pixel-perfect mockups are expensive to change, and change is natural. Do you really want your artists and designers to be in the job of delivering documents? Is it impossible to imagine a tester grabbing a marker and drawing boxes on a whiteboard while talking through a workflow? Does an artist need to always deliver a pixel-perfect mockup, or can they communicate shorthand through an established design language? Have a product owner try roughly drawing a screen on a whiteboard while a programmer writes HTML against established Sass/CSS design patterns. Collaboration encourages a team to gel, and an already experienced team in the right collective headspace will always deliver more quickly when working together.

Waterfall Document Delivery

Don't let your teams only communicate through docs

Product Manager
↓ Requirements deck

Graphic Designer
↓ Pixel-perfect mockups

Developer
↓ Program code

Q/A Tester
↓ Sign-off report

Customer
↓ Support emails

Guide your team to be fully integrated and capable of delivering together. Encourage them do each other's jobs occasionally. Let a tester be a product owner, discovering requirements, because they'll fully explore the product like a customer will. Let programmers manually test, figuring out if their code really does work reliably. Let designers write HTML and CSS ready for programmers to hook up with JavaScript. If they all understand what their teammates do for a living, it helps build up empathy. The next time a task becomes difficult, they might be eager to lend a hand, or at the very least understand why it's tricky and be more sympathetic and accommodating. In a team delivery mentality, no one gets to call something done until it's been fully tested on real devices. When that happens, a feature genuinely is complete and ready to be deployed to web servers for use by customers. When that happens, take a moment to celebrate success together. Have a cheer, ring a bell, and high-five each other. Whatever ceremonies you decide on, embrace them, and have fun.

Serve your teammates. They aren't there for your convenience, but instead, you're there helping them do a better job. Sometimes that attitude drives people to worker harder and dig deeper for one another. I think of it when I'm writing code. I've worked with people who believed they wrote code at work for themselves. They would use their preferred code style and conventions, no matter how terse and cryptic. Now I realize that I write code for my team-mates to read, not the browser, and I optimize for human understanding.

I've read books on personal relationships, and I can't help but reflect on their lessons and apply them to my work situation. Consider this one from Gary Chapman as he meditates on the nature of true love and what it takes to obtain and support it.

> . . . love requires effort and discipline. It is the choice to expend energy in an effort to benefit the other person, knowing that if his or her life is enriched by your effort, you too will find a sense of satisfaction. . .
>
> Gary Chapman, *The 5 Love Languages: The Secret to Love That Lasts*
> (Chicago: Northfield Publishing, 2010, p. 33)

To help with your code's readability, take time to create coding standards for CSS, HTML, and JavaScript before writing any. Write code that looks as if it was written by the same hand. You shouldn't be able to tell who wrote it. At least a file won't look foreign when you crack it open to make a change or take over for a departing coworker. Having a common, well-documented code style is recommended, but what form it takes is up to you. If you want a jumping-off point, please question in your favorite web search engine. Many companies have developed their own styles and written blog articles on the matter. Some have even placed them for public consumption on open-source sites such as GitHub.

Optimistic Outlook

I think most people who work with software engineers think they're pessimistic. They think of what can go wrong as they try writing bug-free code that intelligently handles every known edge-case. In fact, I think engineers are basically optimistic. Technology is so difficult at times that we don't even know what the potential answers are as we start working on a problem, but we always think there is an answer. If it's not found today, then tomorrow is another chance at discovering success. Engineers who don't fundamentally believe that might simply stop coming to work the next day.

At the start of a project, we take time to plan out what needs to be done and spend time trying to ensure nothing goes wrong. That level of control is an illusion, because we'll never fully know what to do until we get into a project. With that in mind, I say that we're artists, designers, and developers, and we're makers. At some point, we must get on with building things. Plan carefully to discover and establish a shared understanding among the team, but then design and code decisively. I find that code working on a device nearly always wins arguments and pushes away doubt.

Creative leaders, please don't cultivate a culture of avoiding failure by heaping on too much process. Favor communication and trust a team that's fully engaged and owns the results. Do whatever you can to guide them toward finding solutions. Encourage your team to meet and reflect on the past few weeks, determining what's working and what's not. Brainstorm potential solutions for what's not working and try some. Will they succeed or fail? Not sure, but it's worth trying and finding out if they become new habits.

Ultimately I judge all code I write by asking if it possesses three simple qualities: Is it functional, is it reliable, and is it simple? Over my career, I've used many languages, operating systems, tools, and hardware kits. What has not changed is my attitude toward mastering my craft, and those three simple qualities are how I evaluate my professional work.

MY PERSONAL POINT OF VIEW

My personal outlook on all of this is that building software is fantastic fun. I love to wake up, learn something new, solve interesting problems, and share what I discover. Websites have always been software, and many are clearly heading in the direction of complex programs. Professional discipline and mastering craft are necessary goals for all of us. That's why I'm eager to deliver a complete box of strong tools to you.

Everything I write comes from slice-of-life experience as an engineer developing websites and web apps alongside artists and designers. All guidance given is written within the context of some problems I've encountered and successfully solved. Furthermore, the chapters will review the challenges and pain points I've realized collaborating with artists and designers. Striving to make this technology real for you and your crew is absolutely important to me. I see hardworking teammates wanting to excel at their work, and it is my honor to serve their needs. When I started my career, I was head down and self-involved in getting my work completed on time. Now I realize that helping others by revealing what I know is a great joy for me.

Tools are always essential to any job. Mastering them is a necessity, because our job is always more difficult than we want it to be. It's creative, it's interactive, we're proud of our effort, and there's never enough time.

Working on the front end of a project feels like home to me. One way or another, it's been the constant focus of my career. I enjoy it because all of my actions are informed by or in the service of a fantastic user experience. It's how I support my customers—by enabling them to better use our software to solve problems. At the end of the day, producing useful work is a satisfying feeling.

Highly collaborative and multidisciplinary teams are a necessity for building today's software, more so than ever because expectations are high and competitors' quality is great. My background building video games showed me that combining programmers, artists, and designers raises everyone's game to a level so high that we could create worlds. Let's do the same things in our industry. Break down skill-based silos and ensure a team is well positioned to start and deliver work together.

Consider ways of having your team members teach one another. Hold instructional lunch-and-learns by area experts. Watch inspirational and informative conference videos. Page through exceptional code together. Bring your pet projects in from home to enlighten one another. Continue investing in each other, raising the potential of everyone. Try each of these things and others and see if they become a part of your culture. Initiate new hires by telling stories of how your team has persevered through challenges and evolved into the successful group it is.

Don't hesitate to pull from the open-source community, but never forget to commit back to it. Support the dedicated volunteers who build the technology from which you benefit. Submit improvements to the source code through GitHub. Blog about how your team uses tech, offering pro tips and tutorials. Publish code snippets answering questions on website forums. Tweet out links to amazing things that you discover. Talk at conferences to educate audiences.

Whenever possible, sell your team on why something has business value, ensure they all understand it well, and then step back. Trust them to make it real and make it better. Listen to them, and remove any blockers when they ask for your help. Hold them accountable for delivering on time.

Overlapping Engineering and Artistry

Why bother learning all this? What's the point of finding out what software engineers do? The fact of the matter is that you and a large percentage of technically minded designers are already doing lots of the things engineers have been doing for their collective history. Activities such as writing programs, maintaining existing source code, and evaluating libraries are traditional core competencies of software engineers. People might try casting your situation in a lesser light, calling it website development, but don't let them make your job feel unimportant.

Historically, pundits might have thought designers and engineers operated at opposite sides of the creative spectrum. One side has people based in numbers and the other has them based in art. Many assume both possess completely incompatible worldviews, and even if they're on the same team, they simply suffer through the day mixed up together. Let's examine the supposed goals of each class of worker. Designers want a website to work well. They might think of the experience of touching a site as much as the delight of looking at it. Engineers want software to work well. They think of it in terms of it being functional, reliable, and simple. How can those two points of view be fundamentally competing? Don't they add up to a more powerful view of the user experience customers want?

It sounds to me as though all the individual needs can be met while working together toward a common goal. If creative leaders are directing their teams toward a full-stack, team-delivery–based effort, why wouldn't all members of the staff desire the same outcome? Strengthening working relationships builds empathy for one another as silos between skillsets start to fall. Negative attitudes of "I have my work done, and I hope you have yours covered" quickly die off. Breeding a candid and supportive culture in which learning, teaching, and openly helping one another makes everyone on the team better. Build capacity to ship more and make the environment more enjoyable.

My goal in writing this book is reviewing many of the most useful skills that I've come to possess. I want to demonstrate the most enabling tools that I've found. I want to empower your emerging mastery with nuts-and-bolts tactics that have helped me succeed throughout my career. This book is dedicated to you if want to elevate your craft and gain productivity by adopting some of the lessons that seem like the exclusive domain of programmers.

I'm an engineer, and I enjoy collaborating with designers. My goal is enlightening you to various programmer-centric tool and techniques. Curious artists wanting to discover more about the technical side of this industry will find they're working more rapidly from learning the techniques and tools clearly explained in this book. You will be introduced to ways of making fact-based decisions and critically debugging your work using tools available from the open-source community and various public-dedicated companies. Following along with the techniques assembled in the book, you'll realize you're more quickly finding problems on your work computer rather than resorting to the inconvenient effort of using production web servers. You can delay purchase of expensive devices such as tablets and phones for finding routine glitches and bugs.

Each chapter feeds upon the last as you build up a complete toolbox of powerful tools. Because building modern websites can quickly become difficult, we reach for tools to reduce frustration and better stay in the iterative creative flow. Staying deeply in that open mode for longer periods of time lets you accomplish profoundly creative work with less effort.

CHAPTER 3

Localhost, the Best Host

How Can We Serve Websites Without Servers?

Is there any way for us to serve a website without a web server? No.

Your business probably already has a web server out on the Internet responding to browser requests right now. This server is "in production" and already dedicated to serving customers. What unexpected craziness might happen if you start making changes to it? Consider the production server unavailable for experimentation. Servers for new projects may not be allocated yet.

Our question then moves away from "How can we view a website without a server?" to "Can we have our own personal web server?" Preferably a server letting us deliver our work as it evolves from design into HTML, JavaScript, CSS, and images, delivered in a meaningful way matching how we'll eventually have it in production.

Is there a way for us to have our own web server? Yes!

A WEB SERVER RUNNING ON YOUR COMPUTER

If we're not putting our website files on a server that's out on the Internet that anyone can browse, does that mean we're faking it somehow? No—we can install the exact same web server software on our own work computers as system administrators do for live production servers housed in data centers. That's a one hundred percent match from our local development environment to final. The only way a critic could claim it's not perfect is by arguing the final configurations are not strictly matching. That's expected and, realistically, not important. What happens in production at scale simply doesn't apply to a localhost setup for an artist, designer, and developer. Of course, it's entirely possible to modify a personal setup over time, if that's useful, but realize it probably won't be.

> A web server on the Internet that anyone can get to is often referred to as "customer facing." That's important enough that we want to ensure it is always available and has the most reliably working files representing our work.

Don't think about prematurely optimizing your server configuration. Customer-facing web servers need to balance large-scale needs, security, performance, and reliability. Your local server doesn't. You just want to critique, polish, validate quality, and test HTML and CSS. Performance tuning a web server is a master craft and worth discovering by interviewing your ops team one day over a tasty drink, but not worth investing your time in to start.

What Localhost Means to Engineers

Software engineers writing back-end server code are using a web server installed on their own computer today, and for years past. It's the truest way to test their work and ensure it's going to behave when pushed out to live production servers. One of the few times engineers don't have their personal web server running is when they have login privileges to a team test computer running a web server. One of these is most likely running inside the company network and often hidden from the public Internet. Jumping to that server through a secure shell allows an engineer control of it at will. This makes a more regimented debugging environment.

Debugging is a key activity for engineers. Because building software at scale is the second most difficult thing that human beings do, it's no surprise that bugs exist. Finding problems under experimentation, then determining the steps for reliably triggering the bugs at will is a key discipline of fixing defective software. Web servers on local computers and shared internal company computers accelerate the bug-finding-and-fixing cycle. You can imagine throwing newly written, barely tested software, up to a public-facing web server is a horrible idea by any measure.

Engineers demand more from their web servers. Artists, designers, and developers might not have the same immediate needs, but it's interesting knowing about them. A few ways to expand a web server are by adding:

- Performance behaviors such as response compression and caching
- Scripting languages such as PHP, Python, and Perl
- Database connectors to MySQL, Oracle, or Postgres
- Security layer such as SSL for HTTPS

As part of testing, I may ask teammates to connect to my personal development web server as it's running my latest work. Connect using what? Sometimes their work browser is fine for simple functional testing. That ability alone will teach us plenty. Mobile emulators such as the Apple iOS Simulator can reach across the company network to hit a computer running a web server. That's surprisingly accurate for measuring up device screen sizes. It'll emulate iPad dimensions as well. Phones and tablets joining the internal Wi-Fi network can hit a development computer for the ultimate test. Running on an actual device is always the best choice for deciding what's really real.

Software engineers have set a precedent that you'll want to follow. Artists and designers are well served to pick up a web server for their own use. It might feel difficult and far from reach, but believe me, it's not. There's a long history of installing, configuring, and maintaining servers that could feel too big to carve up and internalize, but you'll find step-by-step procedures that will help bring this into your digital toolset. You'll want this tool for validating your own work as you build it. You'll want this tool on your own computer, making testing faster with changes confirmed as quickly as you make them.

Artists and designers who have recently started writing HTML, JavaScript, CSS, and other files that look remarkably like code (because they are) will be reaching for web servers for a long time to come. Once you've become empowered with this remarkable tool, you'll feel it's a vibrant addition to your workflow. You'll wonder why you suffered without it for so long. When you begin incorporating it into your daily routine, you'll realize you're working smarter because it offers choices.

HOW LOCALHOST CAN EMPOWER DESIGNERS

Server-side code is executed on a web server. It could be written in languages like Python, PHP, Ruby, or Java, to name a few. Client-side code is executed in a web browser, but the JavaScript, HTML, and CSS files are first sent from that same web server. Designers are writing this client-side code more often than ever before. Surely they will benefit from running their website code and art through their own web server as well.

I specifically suggest that the Apache web server is exactly what you need to integrate into your creative workflow.

The Apache HTTP (web) server is twenty years old, and for the bulk of its lifetime, it surely felt entirely inaccessible to artists and designers. There was absolutely no need to consider it regularly. If a website was up and running, then a web browser brought up a page and that was the extent of an artist's involvement with anything server related. Thinking of installing it was complicated enough to not even bother mentioning. Setting up a web server is usually done automatically by your company's web hosting company or is handled by your system operations teams and software engineers.

> HTTP stands for hypertext transfer protocol. It's the fundamental language of web servers and the simple invention that makes the Internet fun for most viewers. Browsers speak HTTP verbs to a server in order to GET, POST, PUT, or DELETE resources such as JPEG, CSS, HTML, and JavaScript files. This is called a request. In response, a server could send the resource along with a status code. Well-known status codes include 200 (OK) and 404 (NOT FOUND). There are many more response codes, as well as a few more verbs, but these basics will get you started.

The past ten years have brought great advances in websites. As storage space increases, bandwidth costs decrease, and expectations rise. We've seen fantastic advances in websites. High-resolution imagery, highly interactive pages, and complex workflows have defined user experiences as intricate as any traditional desktop program. We might say Apache web server has come into the thoughts of technically minded artists and designers as their user interfaces have added rich detail.

I've found that startup culture is mixing artists and programmers by sitting them side by side in small, open offices. This is fantastic because it casually enables and encourages idea sharing throughout the day. Teammates of each expertise come to understand and appreciate the skills and talents of others. Empathy builds as they witness daily suffering through challenges. Opportunities for cross-training thrive in this style of environment. Artists and designers see tools that engineers have traditionally used, and now they want them.

Having a personal web server on your computer clearly offers a competitive advantage that you'll immediately benefit from as soon as you adopt it. How much of an edge is it? How much better will it make you? It's a range based on how deeply ingrained you make it in your workflow. How much you learn to configure it and realize it as a daily use tool will measure how much it amplifies your skills.

Future artists will do well having a web server installed on their individual work computer. It's not a requirement yet, but designers bringing this productive tool into their daily workflow will possess its significant advantage.

Another good feature of the Apache web server is its "virtual hosts." We'll learn how to set them up in Chapter 4. For now, think of virtual hosts as a feature allowing the same computer to appear as many servers. There are some practical uses past saving the cost of server hardware. For example, every site you want to build source code for can be served up as its own URL. You're familiar with `http://localhost` and `http://127.0.0.1`, but imagine having `http://www.annaspellingwords.local` and `http://www.whatsbeforemobilefirst.local` all accessible on your machine simultaneously. Every virtual site can be tweaked with many settings. Whatever it takes to get closer to the final user experience is worth using during site construction.

Getting closer to the user experience means celebrating the little successes and ensuring that others can see that work, too. We all know having a solid demo ready is key. If someone walks up behind us asking how things are going, will we have something running to show them? I always tell my team to be ready to demo at a moment's notice. Virtual hosts are a good solution for that. When the website is looking fine, make a copy of it. Create a virtual host for it. Give it a name of `http://something_demo.local` and have it always available. No matter how screwy the development gets as you build a site up to awesomeness, that demo version is easily within reach. Let everyone know you have the project under control. Wielding this tool helps.

QUICKLY TURNING AROUND CHANGES

Every creative individual struggles to realize their work by projecting their internal mental image of a thing out into a shared reality via a personal act of creation. Many supportive skills, talents, and tools help accelerate this process. One of the unspoken tools of creativity that I enjoy championing is the particular idea of "flow."

We all know flow when we're in it. It's a unique mental state in which that internalized image of ideal creative form is completely present and all physical effort is in the service of making it real. By the end of the day, it seems work was effortless and time passed by without notice.

If building a website is the creative ideal we want to realize, how does the goal of building it pull you out of the flow? Testing it does. As we want to properly validate our work by putting it on a server and checking it with actual browsers, we have several blockers:

- Asking teammates if a shared test server is available and working properly
- Copying the files up to a server
- Reaching (or searching) for a handheld to view the latest work

Will having a web server installed on your local machine helps you stay in the flow? Unequivocally yes, and let's dig deeper into how it helps you stay in the flow and more quickly turn around changes.

> Handhelds can be emulated various ways on your computer, and we'll cover that in Chapter 8. Having a web server reduces the friction of testing on a device.

The key benefit to having a web server is that it's all yours and patiently awaiting your needs. When it's installed on your computer, there's no sharing and no need to ask around to teammates if you can use it as with a shared testing server. Having files ready for testing means placing them where you tell your server to look. Configuring the server to pull files from your working folder makes testing even more immediate. It's set to go every moment of the day without hesitation and without breaking you away from your creative work flow. It's all yours, and you're the only one it serves.

Dedicated testing staff benefit from this workflow as well. Ensuring quality alongside design invention is entirely possible. Quality assurance (QA) can surely have access to your code by pulling it from a common source-code repository. They can have their own web server to run the latest version. Even if they don't run their own servers, they can work side by side with creative developers, discovering bugs and certainly pointing out problems quickly. It's always cheaper to make changes as early as possible—and undeniably before glitches get out into public view. Changes aren't only creative choices but functional as well. Does the thing you just made work properly? No? Figure out the problem, make a change, and try again.

Leading a creative team and wondering if having a web server is a valuable tool for them? Consider the answer is "yes" and make it your job to follow up with your team to ensure they put time into figuring out how to use it well. Leaders are always searching for ways to fine-tune team delivery. Fine-tune to what effect? Primarily, leaders want to reduce costs and time to market. Incorporating web servers on artist, designer, and developer personal computers is a concrete way to improve and reach that goal.

Don't forget that it's your job as a leader to make sure your team has the time to bring in this tool. Gaining experience with this new tooling means the team is getting more productive, delivering higher quality, and meeting customer needs. Those can be consumer-facing or client expectations. Trading off shorter time to delivery could mean increasing quality. Quality includes creative design polish but also functional "does it work?" evaluation.

FREEDOM! ESCAPING THE TYRANNY OF PRODUCTION SERVERS

Where would be a convenient place to test your work? Production! What are some solid reasons to choose a production server for testing?

- It knows how to serve up a website.
- It's network connected for easy testing.
- Any device can reach it and see how the product looks.
- It's an honest final representation.

Given all those great reasons production is fantastic, we'd never choose to load untested changes on production servers. It'd be insane!

- A CSS file could make all text the wrong color.
- A JavaScript file change could stop a button-click handler.
- A PNG image could double the time it takes for a page to load on mobile.
- We could crash our public-facing product in any number of ways—not cool.

It's admirable to have an eager drive for ensuring our work is fit and working, but our challenge is keeping the production servers reliably up and fully functional. Dumping untested files there would not be helpful toward our primary goal. The fact that production is busy doing important stuff is reason enough to avoiding poking at it. If it crashed, we'd all be sorry.

Those warnings aside, we do need to test our work in as live an environment as possible. That way, when work is pushed to production, we're sure it's good to go. How do we get a safe test version of a live environment? By installing a web server on our personal work computer.

Ideally, we are writing the site's files while we're testing on a web server. Given this total control, more options open up to us for finding mistakes, quirks, and bugs. How do we test? Any way we like. For sure with desktop browsers. Firefox, Chrome, and Internet Explorer are all valid choices. More exciting is the potential for connecting mobile devices to your work computer and hitting the work in progress. That's the awesome we want. Every device we can lay our hands on means one more satisfied customer when our stuff is live in production for all to see.

Designers working on computers with OS X must wonder how to effectively test Internet Explorer. An expert topic is using a "virtual machine" that emulates Windows on your computer. Microsoft has a fantastic solution found at `http://modern.ie`, where you can read about it.

What types of bugs can we expect to see?

- Device specific: the hardware inside phones, tablets, and desktops is different.
- Platform specific: the Android and iOS operating systems are unique.
- Browser specific: Safari, Chrome, and Internet Explorer read code in their own ways.
- Connection type: real-world 3G is slow as compared to the office Wi-Fi.
- Regression: we broke something that was working.

Every test you run lets you gain confidence in your work. Every bug you find is one your audience will never see. Real-world testing with the web server is one of the most powerfully enabling tools that you can toss into your toolbox.

I've come to learn that moving faster is always better, especially when moving with confidence.

IS APACHE WEB SERVER WORTH LEARNING?

In the near future, your peers might ask you why you're learning the Apache web server. You might be asking yourself the same question. Sure, there are alternatives, but none approach its popularity. Look to the next chapter for a list of alternative web servers that you can discover. Please keep in mind that none are obviously better choices for your needs at this point.

Challenging assumptions is always a healthy attitude. For now, let's look at a statistic published in a December 2014 survey published by Netcraft. It specifically measures the Apache web server's popularity.

> *50.57% of all active known websites are running Apache web server.*
> "December 2014 Web Server Survey," last modified December 18, 2014,
> http://news.netcraft.com/archives/2014/12/18/december-2014-web-
> server-survey.html

Once you've internalized and moved past the instruction provided in this book, you'll find a huge active community using the Apache web server. Searching their archives and reaching out to them online and in local user group meetings, you'll find detailed resources for answering your future questions. Rest assured that as you gain experience in applying Apache web server in your day-to-day workflow, you'll become more valuable to your present and future teams, employers, and clients.

The Dream of Seeing What Your Users See

Every time I run my website on my work computer, I know I'm better informed about the user experience I'm creating. Using a desktop browser or pairing up a handheld lets me find quirks I need to fix and sections I want to polish. All of my work is meant for someone to view, and delivering the best effort possible is my goal.

When I'm working without a web server, I always feel as though I'm stumbling in the dark. Making choices based on intuition and guesswork—qualities great for creative moments—is not as good for solving problems. With the array of tools available today, you can see your work as your customers will. You can ship more quickly and go farther with your products than ever before.

It is amazing to say Apache web server is free, because it's incredibly valuable. If you think there's a barrier to entry for installing a web server, if you feel it's stepping outside your comfort zone, don't worry. In the next chapter, you'll find step-by-step directions for installing it on your computer. You may be excited to find out that it's already on your machine. Amazing, right? Depending on your preferred brand of computer, you're only a few steps away from picking up and controlling this instrument.

CHAPTER 4

Apache Web Server

What Server Does Everyone Use?

When we talk about "production servers," what does that mean? What do they do, where are they, and why are they important? How do our customers interact with a production server, and how does it help them? Would it be helpful if we had access to one? Better yet, can we get a server on our own computer so we can see how our work looks in the same way the public does?

Yes.

Without a doubt, we need to have a web server running on the same computer we work on daily. All design work turned into HTML, CSS, JavaScript, and images ought to be seen in a testing environment that's as similar as possible to the production one. Why? Because nothing matters until we confirm our work on customer-facing browsers and the devices they have. Saying "it works on my machine" is super satisfying after a long day of cranking out code, but in the end, it simply doesn't count. Setting up a web server feels difficult, but is it?

No.

A web server is just another tool to grasp with a strong grip and wield with confidence. Anyone feeling it's a challenge should rest assured that the following step-by-step processes will successfully guide you through setup. Pushing past a comfort zone is an opportunity to grow. This experience will raise your professional skills to the next level.

BRIEF INTRODUCTION TO APACHE

The Apache HTTP Server (or simply "Apache") is the most-installed web server software on the Internet today. Why? In its twenty years, it has earned acceptance in the open-source community. Its free cost, frequent updates, patches, optimizations, and security improvements make it an easy choice for system owners, engineers, and designers.

WHERE DO SERVERS LIVE?

When we spin up an Apache web server and copy up our site's files, where does it live? What does it mean to be "in production"? Production is the fully Internet-connected live environment where our customers view the website. Production servers can be in a few places. Each option has trade-offs and benefits, allowing for true choice.

SERVERS ON HARDWARE

Hardware means actual physical computers sitting somewhere. More than likely, they are servers you purchased and mounted in racks that are now sitting in a data center. A data center looks like a warehouse filled with bookshelves (racks) filled with pizza boxes (servers). The cool-looking-blinking-light factor is high in data centers.

Racks are bolted to the floors of a professional data center run by a trained technical staff. What the staff does makes a difference both in action and in price.

- "Managed servers" means they take an active role in monitoring your hardware and software. When any issues are detected, they follow steps scripted in a troubleshooting guide. Steps could include minor maintenance, logging status info, or contacting a teammate who is on call for report and hand-off.

- "Unmanaged servers" means the data center staff basically stays well away from your servers. Their basic guarantee is that your servers pull power and push data across the Internet.

Either way, these servers are devices that you could conceivably drive up to and touch.

SERVERS ON CLOUD COMPUTING

Servers in the cloud are backed by hardware, but not hardware that you need buy. You rent them. Machines are assigned to you on demand from the fleet of servers owned and managed by the cloud service provider. Each server, in fact, is more likely a slice of a commodity server allocated in a matter of minutes of your request. Generally, servers are based on a handful of "off the shelf" sizes along the lines of small, medium, large, and extra large.

The server is selected from a catalog of standard configurations based on operating system and some supporting utilities. From there, you can upload your website files and any additional tools. If you choose this path, find out if your cloud service provider allows for creating a "snapshot" from one of your fully configured servers. From there, it can be added as a configuration choice listed in your private catalog. Choose the snapshot when you ask for a new server. When it spins up, you're ready to rock.

INSTALLING APACHE WEB SERVER ON OS X

The following steps are for installing Apache on Apple's OS X versions 10.8 (Mountain Lion), 10.9 (Mavericks), and 10.10 (Yosemite).

NO NEED TO GET THE INSTALLER

Most installation directions begin with "go download an installer package." No need in this case. One of the distinct advantages of OS X is that Apache comes preinstalled. It's one of the many web tools typically used by programmers that it ships with, such as PHP, Python, and Ruby.

How easy is that? No installation needed, but there is a little setup necessary to activate it.

1.   Open a Terminal window

2.   Type `sudo apachectl start` and enter

3.   Enter your password to confirm administrator privilege

sudo is a program for UNIX-like operating systems (like OS X via Terminal) that feels like a programmer tool but simply means "substitute user do." That's a rather formal idea, but it's generally associated with the most privileged user (e.g., root or administrator). This allows us to tweak files placed in or install files in areas normally restricted by the operating system.

ARE WE DONE? IS APACHE WORKING?

Believe it or not, Apache web server is now running on your work computer. Confirm it's ready by opening your favorite web browser, for example Safari, and entering `http://localhost` in the search bar.

You'll immediately see a simple, confident message: "It works!"

It works!

You did it! You've begun using a tool that's going to make your professional life easier from this day forward. Enjoy a coffee and celebrate this small victory!

> The Internet Protocol address 127.0.0.1 is important because 127 is the last address in the A class of networks and 0.0.1 is the first entry on that network. All requests to 127.0.0.1 are specially interpreted as "loop back to this device," and Apache can catch them. Your localhost is mapped to this address.

Beginning Way to Use the Apache Server

Starting off, Apache has a default folder where all the files making up its website are stored. We can see that via a Finder window.

Open up a Finder and navigate over to the folder that we know Apache installed named /Library/WebServer/Documents. Look for the only file it holds called index.html. Edit the file, seeing it's a single-line document looking like this:

```
<html><body><h1>It works!</h1></body></html>
```

Can we use this same folder to store all of our website work? Will Apache serve our own files to our web browser? Yes! This is the easiest way to get some work done quickly while playing around with your latest development tool.

Congratulations! You own a web server. Shiny! It's worth having some fun playing around with it. When you're ready to raise your game to the next level, come back to the next section. It's worth taking the time to see how you can fine-tune and improve your Apache server to better work for you.

The networking industry uses `localhost` to refer to *this* computer hosting programs and information. It's your "home."

Intermediate Way to Use the Apache Server

Wielding this tool properly means telling Apache where our working folder possessing all of our various website projects is.

1. Launch your favorite text editor for OS X (could be TextWrangler or another one listed in a section that follows)

2. Choose File-> Open and navigate to the folder Apache is installed in by default `/etc/apache2`

Some of these system files may be hidden from view by default. Pressing the keyboard shortcut combination Command-Shift-Period (.) in any open dialog box pop-up shows hidden files.

3. Open the folder inside it called `conf`

4. Open the file called `httpd.conf`

5. Page down and look for the first line we change. It looks like this one, which was line #236 for me:

```
DocumentRoot "/Library/WebServer/Documents"
```

6. Replace the text inside the quotes with a full folder path to your work folder as I have here for mine:

```
Directory "/Users/ken/trees"
```

7. When you begin typing, a dialog box might pop up, asking you, "Are you sure you want to unlock 'httpd.conf'?" because it's a special file. Press the Unlock button as confirmation that you know what's happening.

8. Page down and look for the second line we must change, which looks like this one, which was line #237 for me:

```
<Directory "/Library/WebServer/Documents">
```

9. Replace the text inside the quotes with a full folder path to your work folder as I have here for mine:

```
<Directory "/Users/ken/trees">
```

10. A few lines down is a third one that you must edit from the original install. Find one that looks like this, which was line #250 for me:

```
Options FollowSymLinks Multiviews
```

11. Add the `Indexes` option at the end of the line allowing you to browse directories making it easier to find your work.

```
Options FollowSymLinks Multiviews Indexes
```

12. Save the file and quit your text editor, because you're done with the changes. A dialog box might pop up asking you, ". . . wants to make changes. Type your password to allow this." Do so, and click the Allow button to give permission.

13. That was simple, right? There are lots of hardcore-looking settings in that configuration file that quickly get technical. No need to touch them for now—or ever, unless you want to specifically learn more about them one day.

14. Restart the Apache web server by opening a Terminal window. Type `sudo apachectl restart`, which restarts the Apache server. Give it a minute to turn itself off and back on again. Let it forget about the old settings and read in the new ones you've just changed in `httpd.conf`.

```
[~]-> sudo apachectl restart
Password:
[~]->
```

15. Open your web browser and navigate to `http://localhost` once again. What ought to be different is you're seeing a list of folders in your working folder. For example, I have a folder in my personal account called `trees` that holds each of my projects. Clicking on any folder showing in your web browser will launch the `index.html` found inside it. If not found, Apache shows a list of files and folders it discovers. Explore until you find your project's starting point.

Index of /

Name	Last modified	Size	Description
AnnaSpellingWords/	06-Apr-2014 19:32	-	
BookDeal/	08-Apr-2014 20:11	-	
JasmineTestingBackBo..>	15-Dec-2013 11:02	-	
KATzCool2/	02-Apr-2014 22:31	-	
MadeFreshCoffee/	15-Dec-2013 10:58	-	
Responsizer.js/	06-Oct-2013 10:12	-	
S3DeployJS/	26-Jan-2014 22:28	-	

With this change, you have a web server that I'm confident will meet your needs for a long time to come. You've already brought a tool into your workflow that will boost your productivity by catching errors before they get out to your customers. Furthermore, this tool will be a platform that you can enhance over time.

One more change you might like to make is covered in the next section for advanced use. Changing more configuration files lets you get even closer to the production world and set up an expert work environment. It's not important for now, however.

Installing Apache on Windows

Installing Apache on Windows begins with simply downloading a single setup file from the project's website. Some people expect it's more complicated than that given how important web servers are, but in fact, it's only a program like any other. Plenty of smart people went through the challenge of building it to make our lives easier. We're going to take advantage of that starting now.

LET'S GO GET THE SETUP FILE

1.   Open up your favorite web browser and navigate over to `http://httpd.apache.org`

Essentials

- About
- License
- FAQ
- Security Reports

Download!

- From a Mirror

Documentation

- Version 2.4
- Version 2.2
- Version 2.0
- Trunk (dev)
- Wiki

The Number One HTTP Server On The Internet

The Apache HTTP Server Project is an effort to develop and maintain an open-source HTTP server for modern operating systems including UNIX and Windows NT. The goal of this project is to provide a secure, efficient and extensible server that provides HTTP services in sync with the current HTTP standards.

Apache httpd has been the most popular web server on the Internet since April 1996, and celebrated its 17th birthday as a project this February.

The Apache HTTP Server ("httpd") is a project of The Apache Software Foundation.

Apache httpd 2.4.9 Released	2014-03-17

The Apache Software Foundation and the Apache HTTP Server Project are pleased to announce the release of version 2.4.9 of the Apache HTTP Server ("Apache"). This version of Apache is our latest GA release of the new generation 2.4.x branch of Apache HTTPD and represents fifteen years of innovation by the project, and is recommended over all previous

2.   Click on "Download! From a Mirror"

Essentials

- About
- License
- FAQ
- Security Reports

Download!

- From a Mirror

Documentation

- Version 2.4
- Version 2.2
- Version 2.0
- Trunk (dev)
- Wiki

Downloading the Apache HTTP Server

Use the links below to download the Apache HTTP Server from one of our mirrors. You **must** verify the integrity of the downloaded files using signatures downloaded from our main distribution directory.

Only current recommended releases are available on the main distribution site and its mirrors. Older releases, including the 1.3 family of releases, are available from the archive download site.

Stable Release - Latest Version:

- 2.4.9 (released 2014-03-17)

Legacy Release - 2.2 Branch:

- 2.2.27 (released 2014-03-26)

3.   Look for the section "Stable Release" and click on the version ("2.4.9" as of the time of this writing)

- Flood
- libapreq
- Modules
- mod_fcgid
- mod_ftp

Miscellaneous

- Contributors
- Sponsors
- Sponsorship

Apache HTTP Server 2.4.9 (httpd): 2.4.9 is the latest available version

The Apache HTTP Server Project is pleased to announce the release of version 2.4.9 of the Apache HTTP Server ("Apache" and "httpd"). This version of Apache is our latest GA release of the new generation 2.4.x branch of Apache HTTPD and represents fifteen years of innovation by the project, and is recommended over all previous releases!

For details see the Official Announcement and the CHANGES_2.4 and CHANGES_2.4.9 lists

- Source: httpd-2.4.9.tar.bz2 [PGP] [MD5] [SHA1]

- Source: httpd-2.4.9.tar.gz [PGP] [MD5] [SHA1]

- Binaries

- Security and official patches

- Other files

Apache HTTP Server 2.2.27 (httpd)   2014-03-26

The Apache HTTP Server Project is pleased to announce the release of Apache HTTP Server (httpd) version 2.2.27.

4.   Click on the "binaries" entry to see what's available for download

Index of /apache//httpd/binaries

Name	Last modified	Size	Description
Parent Directory		-	HTTP Server project
netware/	24-Mar-2014 07:30	-	HTTP Server project
win32/	17-Nov-2013 08:14	-	HTTP Server project
README.html	17-Nov-2013 08:23	1.1K	HTTP Server project

Download from your **nearest mirror site!**

Please do not download from www.apache.org. Use a mirror site to help us save apache.org bandwidth and to speed up your download. Click here to find your nearest mirror.

Apache HTTP Server binary builds

This directory contains contributed binary builds from committers, when available for a given platform.

5.   Click on "win32/" folder

6.   Scroll down to the file list and look for the filename with the latest version number and ending with the `.msi` extension. I found this one: `httpd-2.2.25-win32-x86-no_ssl.msi`.

Name	Last modified	Size	Description
Parent Directory		-	HTTP Server project
patches_applied/	23-Aug-2012 20:25	-	Official patches
symbols/	10-Jul-2013 01:07	-	HTTP Server project
HEADER.html	03-Oct-2009 15:02	631	HTTP Server project
LEGACY.html	05-Mar-2010 18:24	5.6K	HTTP Server project
README.html	17-Nov-2013 08:14	10K	HTTP Server project
TROUBLESHOOTING.html	03-Oct-2009 15:02	2.7K	HTTP Server project
httpd-2.0.65-win32-x86-no_ssl.msi	10-Jul-2013 01:06	4.8M	MSI Installer Package
httpd-2.0.65-win32-x86-openssl-0.9.8y.msi	10-Jul-2013 01:06	5.5M	MSI Installer Package
httpd-2.2.25-win32-x86-no_ssl.msi	10-Jul-2013 01:06	5.5M	MSI Installer Package
httpd-2.2.25-win32-x86-openssl-0.9.8y.msi	10-Jul-2013 01:06	6.1M	MSI Installer Package
mod_fcgid-2.3.6-win32-x86.zip	06-Nov-2010 05:49	116K	HTTP Server project
mod_ftp-0.9.6-beta-win32-x86.zip	08-Oct-2009 23:11	154K	HTTP Server project

Download from your nearest mirror site!

www.trieuvan.com/apache//httpd/binaries/win32/httpd-2.2.25-win32-x86-no_ssl.msi

7.   Save that file.

INSTALLING THE SERVER

1.   Double-click the Apache installer app icon

2.   Press the "Run" button if Windows asks if the `.msi` installer is okay for use. It's simply a safety check that we know is fine.

3.   Click on the "Next" button when the "Welcome to the Installation Wizard for Apache" dialog box shows

Welcome to the Installation Wizard for Apache HTTP Server 2.2.25

The Installation Wizard will install Apache HTTP Server 2.2.25 on your computer. To continue, click Next.

WARNING: This program is protected by copyright law and international treaties.

| < Back | Next > | Cancel |

4.   Read through the "License Agreement" as you like, pressing the "Next" button

5.   Read through the "Read This First" text as you like, pressing the "Next" button

6.   Look for the Server Information dialog box, pressing the "Next" button after typing
      these values for each entry:
      a.   Network Domain: `localhost`
      b.   Server Name: `localhost`
      c.   Administrator's Email Address: `admin@localhost`

Server Information

Please enter your server's information.

Network Domain (e.g. somenet.com)

localhost

Server Name (e.g. www.somenet.com):

localhost

Administrator's Email Address (e.g. webmaster@somenet.com):

admin@localhost

Install Apache HTTP Server 2.2 programs and shortcuts for:

⦿ for All Users, on Port 80, as a Service -- Recommended.

◯ only for the Current User, on Port 8080, when started Manually.

InstallShield

[< Back]   [Next >]   [Cancel]

7.   Click "Typical" on the "Setup Type" dialog box and press the "Next" button

Setup Type

Choose the setup type that best suits your needs.

Please select a setup type.

◉ **Typical**

Typical program features will be installed. (Headers and Libraries for compiling modules will not be installed.)

○ **Custom**

Choose which program features you want installed and where they will be installed. Recommended for advanced users.

InstallShield ————————————————————————————————————

[< Back]   [Next >]   [Cancel]

8.   When the "Destination Folder" dialog box shows, press the "Change" button and select somewhere else

Destination Folder

Click Change to install to a different folder

Install Apache HTTP Server 2.2 to the folder:

C:\Program Files (x86)\Apache Software Foundation\Apache2.2\   [Change...]

InstallShield ————————————————————————————————————

[< Back]   [Next >]   [Cancel]

9. Change the destination folder to something visible and easily found later—for example, `C:\Apache2.2`

Change Current Destination Folder

Browse to the destination folder.

Look in:

| 🏠 Apache2.2 | ▼ | 📁 | 📁 |

    💾 Local Disk (C:)
      🏠 Apache2.2
    💾 Local Disk (D:)
    📀 DVD RW Drive (E:)

Folder name: (Note that backslashes are required, use C:\Path, not C:/Path)

`C:\Apache2.2\`

InstallShield ————————————————————————————————————

    [OK]   [Cancel]

---

10. Press the "Next" button

11. Click the "Install" button at the "Ready to Install the Program" dialog box

Ready to Install the Program

The wizard is ready to begin installation.

Click Install to begin the installation.

If you want to review or change any of your installation settings, click Back. Click Cancel to exit the wizard.

InstallShield ————————————————————————————————————

    [< Back]   [**Install**]   [Cancel]

12.   Allow the setup process to copy all the files into place

13.   Look for the "Installation Wizard Completed" dialog box and press "Finish"

ARE WE DONE? IS APACHE WORKING?

Fantastic! Now the Apache web server is fully prepared. In fact, it's already running as you're reading these words. As part of setup installation, it's placed on your computer and running in the background. When you reboot your machine, you'll find Apache running and ready once again, serving up your website as you build it.

How do we know for a fact that Apache web server is running on our work machine? Two important ways come to mind:

- Apache shows a notification icon down in the taskbar area running along the bottom edge of the desktop. The icon looks like a red feather stuck into a white disc holding a green arrow. A label entitled "Running all Apache services" pops up when a mouse hovers above it.

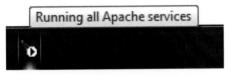

- Browse your new server! Open a web browser (for example, Internet Explorer) and in the address bar type `127.0.0.1` and then press enter. You ought to see the default Apache web page cheerfully report, "It works!"

It works!

The Internet Protocol address `127.0.0.1` is important because 127 is the last address in the A class of networks and `0.0.1` is the first entry on that network. All requests to `127.0.0.1` are specially interpreted as "loop back to this device," and Apache can catch them.

Beginning Way to Use the Apache Server

In the previous section, we navigated to our localhost server with a web browser and saw the reassuring "It works!" placeholder page. This default page is an index.html file stored in one of the folders Apache installed. Let's have a look at where that is and what that file looks like.

Open up a File Explorer and navigate over to the folder where you told Apache to install. For example, type `C:\Apache2.2` if you used that while following along in the previous installing section.

Open a folder called `htdocs` and look for the only file held there called `index.html`. Edit the file, seeing it's a single-line document looking like this:

```
<html><body><h1>It works!</h1></body></html>
```

Can we use this same folder to store all of our website work? Will Apache serve up our own files to our web browser? Yes! Surely this is the easiest way to get some work done quickly while playing around with your latest development tool.

Congratulations! You now own a web server. Shiny! It's worth having some fun playing around with it. When you're ready, come back to the next section when you want to raise your game a level. It's worth taking the time to see how you can fine-tune and improve your Apache server to better work for you.

htdocs is an abbreviation for "hypertext documents," which refers to the original idea of authors relating supportive materials to one another by quickly followed connections. Now it's so commonplace to "click on a link" that we rarely think of it, but back in the day, it was a significant invention.

Intermediate Way to Use the Apache Server

You've already seen in the previous section that you have an Apache web server running. Your localhost is working, and it's a fantastic tool that will serve you well. If you're using it, your website pages will come up looking more like how they will in a live production environment. Empathy is a strong tool, and this lets you see your work nearly the same way your customers eventually will.

Because the Apache server is running and serving up your files, you may find the next section isn't absolutely necessary for getting work done. True, but I believe it's helpful for adjusting the tool to better fit your work life.

Does it feel as though moving your files in the Apache folder is inflexible and leads to extra effort? I agree. What I do instead of moving my work is teach Apache where my working folder is. Then it can look for and serve files from there.

For example, as part of my workflow, I keep a folder called `d:\trees`, where all my various project folders live. If I tell Apache to consider that its document folder, then I easily access all my past and current projects. It's perfect!

Teaching Apache where our work folder is means updating one of the files it created during installation. It's a text file full of its various settings called a "configuration file." We'll change the file in two places and restart the server, letting it switch over. Then we'll have a coffee and admire our work.

1. Open a File Explorer and click on the folder you installed Apache into—for example, `C:\Apache2.2` if you used that while following the installing section

2. Double-click into the `conf` folder

Organize ▼	Include in library ▼	Share with ▼	Burn	New folder		▦ ▼	▣	❷
★ Favorites	**Name**	**Date modified**	**Type**	**Size**				
	📁 extra	4/2/2014 7:25 PM	File folder					
📚 Libraries	📁 original	4/2/2014 7:25 PM	File folder					
	📄 charset.conv	4/2/2014 7:25 PM	CONV File	2 KB				
📡 Homegroup	📄 httpd.conf	4/2/2014 7:25 PM	Text Document	18 KB				
	📄 magic	4/2/2014 7:25 PM	File	14 KB				
🖥 Computer	📄 mime.types	4/2/2014 7:25 PM	TYPES File	54 KB				
💾 Local Disk (C:)								
💿 Local Disk (D:)								
🌐 Network								

6 items

3. Open the file called `httpd.conf` with a text editor of your choice (could be Notepad or another one listed in a section that follows)

4. Page down and look for the first line we change. It looks like this one, which was line #236 for me

```
DocumentRoot "c:/Apache2.2/htdocs"
```

5. Replace the text inside the quotes with a full folder path to your work folder, as I have here for mine:

```
DocumentRoot "d:\trees"
```

6. Page down and look for the second line we must change. It looks like this one, which was line #237 for me:

```
<Directory "C:/Apache2.2/htdocs">
```

7. Replace the text inside the quotes with a full folder path to your work folder, as I have here for mine:

```
<Directory "d:\trees">
```

8. Save the file and quit your text editor, because you're done with the changes.

9. That was simple, right? There are lots of hardcore-looking settings in that configuration file that quickly get technical. No need to touch them for now—or ever, unless you want to specifically learn more about them one day.

10. Restart the Apache server. Remember that red arrow notification icon in the taskbar area that we saw earlier? Right click on it and select the "Restart" option. Give it a few minutes to turn itself off and back on again. Let it forget about the old settings and read in the new ones you've just changed in `httpd.conf`.

11. Open your web browser and navigate to `127.0.0.1` once again. What ought to be different is you're seeing a list of folders in your working folder. For example, I have a folder in `d:\trees` for each of my projects. Clicking on a folder will launch the

`index.html` found inside it. If not found, Apache shows a list of files and folders it discovers. Explore until you find your project's starting point.

Index of /

- AnnaTeaching/
- JasmineTestingBackBoneModel/
- KATzCool2/
- MadeFreshCoffee/
- Responsizer.js/
- TStringJS/
- desktop.ini

With this change, you have a web server that I'm confident will meet your needs for a long time to come. You've already brought a tool into your workflow that will boost your productivity by catching errors before they get out to customers. Furthermore, this tool will be a platform that you can enhance over time.

One more change you might like to make is covered in the next section for "advanced" use. Changing more configuration files lets you get even closer to the production world and set up an expert work environment. It's not important for now, however.

> The networking industry uses `localhost` to refer to *this* computer hosting programs and information. It's your "home."

Advanced Way to Use Localhost Apache Web Server

Considering this chapter outlined beginning and intermediate ways to use Apache web server, you must be wondering what's next. What's the "advanced" way to use this new power tool that we're bringing into our workflow? We'll save details on the next level of Apache for later just to keep life a bit simper as you concentrate on living with this tool for a while longer. Take time to practice with it as you know it now. It will serve you well. Gain confidence configuring it, starting and stopping it, and generally becoming your local authority on the tool.

When you're ready, flip forward to Chapter 6, where "Virtual Hosts" are covered. It contains what I consider to be the advanced-level knowledge for this book's audience. That chapter shows you how to have your local web server run in a way that mimics multiple web servers. Each virtual web server is set to deliver one of your folders full of the source code that makes a particular website. When you get to that point, you'll find it's useful to have multiple virtual servers running on your single computer.

Each virtual server can have its own hostname just like any website on the Internet does. Using virtual servers in this way makes them feel more real and, in turn, helps you deliver more convincing demos to your clients to enable them to give more detailed feedback. It also helps you discover missing details that you need to complete before launching the site to a public-facing server.

HINTING AT FUTURE CONFIGURATIONS

Of course, web servers don't stop at serving up website files such as .HTML, .CSS, .JPG, and .JS. You could extend your localhost server with various additions, making it even more capable of comparing to live environments. Especially interesting are programming languages or setting upgrades. These optional modules can include:

- PHP, Python, and Perl scripting languages
- SSL security
- Resource cache control
- Support of new MIME file types
- MySQL database

None of these is the least bit important to you at this moment. You're at the early steps of incorporating this powerful tool into your daily workflow and ought to be completely satisfied at that progress. Spending time using Apache to serve up your website project is entirely the best use of your time.

Investing more time in looking into the details of the `httpd.conf` file isn't worth it yet. Is it worth doing in the future? Possibly. It surely would open up another level of power to you, but more than likely, this will happen when pairing up with a back-end software engineer. When a designer pushes to the next level, integrating his or her front-end pages with an engineer's back-end server layer, that's a whole new level of spectacular. Think of that now, explore potential in the future, and take it on once you have confidence and have mastered your current potential.

Brief Tour of Text Editors

Why are text editors specifically called out as special? It's because certain programs, like we've already seen with Apache in this chapter, offer special ways of changing their behavior through "configuration files." The only way they work is when the configuration file is purely text. No special formatting is needed or allowed. No need to mark text in italics or with colors or with special composition as a word processor might.

Reading and writing files made up purely of text is when programmers reach for text editors. In fact, they're used by programmers so often that this category of tools is referred to as "programmer editors." By now you've chosen one for your own.

What types of files do we recognize as pure text? Plenty. Of course, you know several very well by now: HTML, CSS, and JavaScript. It's no coincidence that they are text considering they consist of program code. Pictures that you've made in .JPG, .PNG, and .GIF format are not text files. They are referred to as "binary files." The information stored within them consists of numbers specifically interpreted by viewing programs as pictures. Opening a binary picture file in a text editor will partially reveal its insides. Generally they'll look like messy junk. Don't be surprised if they beep at you a bit.

For good times, casually ask a group of software engineers, "What's your favorite programming editor?" Take a step back and watch where the debate goes. Lots of times it's a good conversation as a highly opinionated group with a strong stance on the matter banters back and forth. Why is it such a big deal for a programmer? Because text editors are a daily-use tool. Furthermore, it's a constant touchpoint, and there are enough choices with strong opinions by their makers that committed ideas exist on the matter. Feature-rich text editors make programmers more productive, and they ought to know them well.

Productivity springs from the features making text editors truly a unique tool over word processors. Both seem similar, but in fact, once you deeply learn how to wield a text editor, you'll find its power. Text editors help far past editing an Apache server configuration file, because it's a daily touchpoint for crafting source code for your websites. Prepare to have a text editor boost your ability to write JavaScript, HTML, and CSS. These are the ways you can better wield your text editor:

- Learn the hotkeys to accelerate your experience of moving text around and navigating through your files.
- Seek out and snap in plug-ins to extend your capabilities.
- Customize fonts, color themes, and layout for your personal preference.

If going on about this subject seems humorous to you, believe me that it can be when the proper mix of stubborn people start comparing notes. What's even more fantastic is that you'll form your own strongly held belief on the matter soon enough. All I can say is that professional makers need tools, and those become extensions of them and, in turn, shape their outlook and attitude. Pride in craft is never a bad thing. Stand up for what you believe in, have opinions, but be ready to learn while you're sharing.

You may be happy with the text editor that comes with your computer, but I encourage you to go out and choose a few to sample. Work with them and see which fits your style and budget. Listed next are a few highlights for each system, but there are many more choices to discover. Learn by reading reviews of them through web searches, interviewing teammates, or asking at local meetups. Some text editors are free to use forever. Others offer free evaluation time before deciding to buy.

TEXT EDITORS ON OS X

Here are a few well-known text editors that run on OS X computers.

- TextWrangler
- Sublime Text
- TextMate
- Atom
- Brackets
- BBEdit

If any of your software engineer buddies tell you to use a text editor called VIM, run away. It's the sort of low-level tool that hardcore UNIX-heads love to use. It's cryptic on purpose, running on the command line, revealing nothing about itself. Looking at it makes me think it's the working definition of an anti-user interface. It does work well in this situation, and it's built into OS X, making it an obvious choice to reach for. Instead, look for its equally useful but slightly more self-revealing "nano." It runs in a Terminal, and you can edit an Apache configuration file like this:

1. Open a Terminal window
2. Type `sudo nano /etc/apache2/httpd.conf` and enter
3. Enter your password to confirm administrator privilege

TEXT EDITORS ON WINDOWS

Here are a few well-known text editors that run on Windows computers.

- NotePad++
- Sublime Text
- Brackets
- Atom
- UltraEdit

Stopping Apache Web Server

You might be wondering, now that you finally have Apache web server running, why would we talk about stopping it? That's a fine question, and I agree. This was a question that came up from an attendee after I gave a conference talk reviewing these tools. The attendee happily told me that he followed along with my presentation and executed the steps on his machine as I reviewed from my projected slides. He told me he is the type of technically minded designer that I hope to empower, and he literally never knew how easy it was to run Apache on his OS X laptop. He had it running inside the start and stop of my 45-minute session. Of course, I couldn't have been more proud of him and satisfied that I served my community.

Still, he wondered how to stop Apache, and I hadn't covered it, but I'll list it here. From my perspective, there's no need to stop Apache, but admittedly, it's my point of view. When Apache is installed and started, it writes to a little configuration file in the operating system that "flips a switch" so that it can rise up and run on reboot. The goal here is the convenience that developers, designers, and engineers will have their system ready to rock starting each day of work.

Asking to turn off Apache might simply be a matter of habit that we've all learned since childhood. You'll recognize one of these messages that comes to my mind: "Clean up after yourself," "Waste not, want not," and "Tear down after testing." Considering those memes kicking around in my brain, I can't blame the enthusiastic attendee for asking me how to turn off Apache.

Someone might be a bit security conscious and want to be sure their work in progress isn't something others around them can see. That's a real daily consideration for contractors and for developers in government-related offices. Realistically speaking, Apache running in the background doesn't take up many resources from your operating system or hardware in comparison to image editors, programming editors, or streaming music players.

Whatever the point of view, we will review how to stop Apache. Practicing it surely enhances our knowledge of this tool all the more.

STOPPING THE SERVER ON OS X

Once Apache server is running, it keeps running, even on reboot, until you command it to stop. Here's how you do it.

1.   Open a Terminal window

2.   Enter `sudo apachectl stop`

```
[~]-> sudo apachectl stop
Password:
[~]->
```

3.   Enter your password to confirm administrator privilege

Now Apache web server is stopped. This is easily confirmed. Open up a web browser of your choice, for example Safari, and aim it at `localhost` and watch the response. It ought to report back a generic message of the idea "Cannot connect to the server."

Safari Can't Connect to the Server

Safari can't open the page "localhost" because Safari can't connect to the
server "localhost".

STOPPING THE SERVER ON WINDOWS

When you install and start running Apache web server, it will continue running even across reboots. Stopping it takes a few point and clicks.

1. Remember that Apache shows a notification icon down in the taskbar area running along the bottom edge of the desktop. The icon looks like a red feather stuck into a white disc holding a green arrow. Click on it to see a pop-up of choices.

2. Select Apache2.2 and see its submenu list

	Start
	Stop
☀ Apache2.2 ▶	Restart

3. Select Stop

Now Apache web server is deactivated, and it's "flipped off the switch," telling Windows it's not going to run again on reboot. If you want to confirm that Apache is no longer running, simply open up a web browser of your choice, for example Internet Explorer, and point it at `127.0.0.1`. What you see in response ought to be a typical generic message along the lines of "The webpage cannot be found."

The webpage cannot be found

HTTP 404

Most likely causes:
- There might be a typing error in the address.
- If you clicked on a link, it may be out of date.

What you can try:

● Retype the address.

● Go back to the previous page.

● Go to and look for the information you want.

⊙ More information

OS X Upgrades Can Bring Apache Web Server Changes

Upgrading your OS X operating system generally brings along an upgraded version of Apache Web Server since it's bundled into the package. Upgrades are good because they bring routine enhancements, optimizations, and bug fixes that you'll want to use. Upgrades can be confusing for a few moments because your setup will apparently stop working. Configuration changes that you made while editing `httpd.conf` will be overwritten with the latest default values during the upgrade process.

When you upgrade OS X, and it seems as though Apache Web Server has changed back to its default file serving behavior, recognize it's time to redo any changes you've made to `httpd.conf`.

You might get an early hint that something is going on based on writing and chatting from people you follow online. Another source of help will be found on this book's companion website `http://www.hammeringresponsivewebdesign.com`. Use it as a guide to help you work through upgrade events to quickly return to working order.

Alternatives to Apache

You now know how to install and run the Apache HTTP web server. You'll quickly find it to be a key technology in your toolbox for hammering responsive web design into shape. Chapters 5 and 6 introduce new ways for you to extend your use of the Apache web server.

Human nature always makes us wonder, "Is there another way?" In this case, is there another way to install Apache? Is there another type of web server?

ALTERNATIVES—PACKAGED INSTALLERS

At first, installing a web server seemed intimidating and out of reach, but now you have yours running well and are getting comfortable using it. Some of your colleagues might think installing it by hand feels too difficult and beyond their comfort level. How will you counsel them? They might ask if there's a simpler way to install Apache.

There are alternative ways to install Apache. Certain "all in one" bundles seek to install Apache as well as extra features not yet important to us. What types of features? Examples are a server-side language for business logic and a database for storing user data. Rest assured that because you have installed Apache now, these additional elements could be installed in the future if needed.

Private companies and open communities maintain bundled installers. If someone wants to use one of these bundled packages and asks for your help, explore these keywords in your favorite search engine to learn more:

- "LAMP"—an acronym for Linux, Apache, MySQL, and PHP
- "WAMP"—an acronym for Windows, Apache, MySQL, and PHP
- "XAMPP"—an acronym representing "X" operating system, Apache, MySQL, PHP, and Perl

I want to deliver a word of warning to you as we review this subject. One of my designer colleagues showed me a packaged installer he used. It was recommended by one of his off-site developers. I'll assume the advice was given with good intentions to get his design partner going, but in fact, it limited him. The packaged installer offered an easily used interface that specified what website folder is served up by localhost. The problem is that the seductively easy-to-use GUI only provided a single active folder and therefore only one website available at once. That's terribly weak given what you've already seen in this chapter. We can do much better than a single directory and website at once.

When you're looking at these, you might ask, "Are these really easier than what I did earlier?" That's a fair reaction, and the answer is "yes" only if you need to solve the problem they're built for—installing many things at once. Do you need that problem solved? Not so far.

ALTERNATIVES TO APACHE WEB SERVER

Apache web server remains the most popular selection for hosting and serving web files. There are enough alternatives that we have a real choice. Why would we choose an alternative if Apache works fine? Sometimes it's just a matter of taste. Each has its own profile of awesome that might compel one team to reach for it on their project.

More often than not, this is a choice made by teams spinning up the customer-facing servers. Live production environments may have certain unique needs that we creators do not. Apache will be the best fit for the overriding majority of us for a long time to come.

Server	Key Benefits
Nginx	Quickly serves "static" web pages, lightweight and intentionally kept lean, portable running across many operation systems
lighttpd	High-capacity with an eye toward scaling, lightweight and intentionally kept lean, portable running across many operation systems
Internet Information Server (IIS)	Microsoft made and well integrated with their technology ecosystem, concentration on administration tools, enterprise friendly

Although you can plainly see these choices exist, please understand this is an advanced topic that I won't ask you to put too much thought into. Simply treat this as a "nice to know" item. By asking around and through reading articles, you will discover more servers exist.

Many are highly focused concentrating on solving particular problems such as a specific type of file, offering an operational behavior, or linked inside a specific type of technology. More than likely, you'll never need to make that choice. Instead, a network operations team as part of a larger company will evaluate and adopt that server.

Apache + Laptop = Localhost #Joy

This is an exciting time! Successfully installing and configuring this software has elevated your skills above those around you. Feel free to keep your knowledge for your own advantage, or share it in the spirit of serving your team and community.

Software engineers have used Apache web servers for a long time, and now you've caught up with them. How will you soon surpass them?

Having a web server at your disposal, conveniently running on your working laptop, is rapidly becoming a commonplace necessity. It's a pragmatic tool for confirming work, validating assumptions, and catching problems before delivering a design into customer-facing production servers.

CHAPTER 5

Connecting Devices to Your Computer

Grab a Phone and Go

In the previous chapter, you invested a good amount of time installing Apache web server on your work computer. By now, everyone you know ought to be sick and tired of your proudly showing off localhost. This includes but is not limited to your teammates, supervisor, clients, parents, spouse, friends, and random people at the coffee shop. Each and every one of them should know how amazing it is having one's own web server. Each of them ought to shudder when they see you walking toward them with your laptop in hand and a silly grin across your face as you look to catch their attention for another demo of what's new.

Of course, you understand this tool is positively astounding. Because you've integrated the Apache web server into your workflow, you know the tool is a fantastic productivity boost. You'll see more opportunities to polish your work to a higher quality level. You'll discover and squish more bugs than ever before. You can use any of the popular web browsers to view your website. Because of that, you'll generally witness your work come alive in an environment more real than ever before. How can you push your work to an even more faithful environment?

By getting your website running on your phones and tablets.

Our mobile phones have web browsers just as our work computer does. Using them to hit our localhost makes Apache serve our work in progress for critique on the exact same devices we want and need to prove function. Responsive web development is very much about handling a world of device shapes, and we must seek validation on hardware whenever possible. I've found I never have enough devices for testing my work. That constraint is an obvious limitation for all of us with limited budgets. Even so, judging our work on our own phones and tablets within arm's reach is confidence building.

This chapter shows you how to connect typical phones and tablets to your work machine. It will be easier than you can imagine and more constructive than you might hope.

Testing Localhost Website on Real Mobile Devices

When I was making video games, we always had ways of emulating the physical video game system. It was often the only option we had as teams of engineers as the big console companies were finalizing their hardware designs. Software had to be ready to launch the same day the boxed systems went on sale, meaning "make it work" was our inspirational mantra. We were smart about it and never reached too far past target specifications and scheduled capacities. The worst thing that could happen was overbuilding a game world. Densely packing a terrain with overly detailed characters, loading it with inanimate objects, and mixing in visual effects always made impressive-looking demos. If final hardware couldn't run that amount of detail, we cried. We cried and worked late making huge changes to our game worlds, chopping out stuff until it ran on final hardware.

The video game industry demands cutting-edge performance, stunning visuals, and precise user control at high frame rates. Does that challenge sound familiar to you? Loading up a website with every visual detail specified in CSS3 puts a demand on modern browsers. Rounded corners, drop shadows, text effects, transparency, and background fills are a complicated rendering mix for any modern browser. Worse yet, our phones might not have a cutting-edge browser or capable hardware.

For a long time, and still to this day with legacy Android phones, there are two web browsers available. Sadly, the wrong one is default, and that's obvious when the choice is a generic globe icon titled "Internet." This is generally the slower, more obsolete web browser. Its rendering algorithms are the oldest and least optimized and may not understand cell phones with hardware-accelerated graphics coprocessors. Recently made hardware is capable of doing two things at once: the "thinking" and computing that go on in the main CPU and the "drawing" that goes on in the graphics chip. It's easy to imagine that this low-end browser is running on an equally low-end phone lacking that hardware. All of that adds up for a nasty user experience.

Cell phones can be relatively slow turning on the cell radio, making requests to web servers for assets, and dragging them over the air. They're laughably slow compared to your Wi-Fi–connected desktop computer. Image assets may even be requested twice. That happens in the case that transmission is interrupted long enough to abandon the download. For a fun time, see if you can make this happen by walking around your office building while hitting websites. Observe how fast they come down and how long it takes for first page render. Find out if some hallways are faster than others depending on how near a window you are. How can we predict that? We can't. We can only intelligently plan ahead to minimize the impact.

Google's open-source mobile operating system, Android, is popular with device manufacturers because they can take and tweak it to their needs. In practice, I've found devices from different brands render my web pages differently. Differences even occur when comparing two devices having a different "point release" of the same major operating system number. I've learned to test my website on everything I can put my hands on before launch. Simply testing on a single Android device doesn't guarantee your website will look great on all Android powered hardware.

Fingers are less precise than mouse pointers. Bigger, too. Mobile screens under sunlight look washed out compared to desktop monitors in a perfectly ambient-lit office. There's no hover state. Breakpoints aren't where you expect. Some tablets have aspect ratios shaped more like a theater screen than a computer monitor. It's all kinds of crazy, and keeping it sorted out in our heads like some sage-like visionary dispensing answers to eager teammates is a sure way to insanity. Many people, including me, call on responsive web design as a way to cope with varied hardware sizes. Responsive design and development is a physical activity best put on our sketchbooks, on our text editors, and onto devices.

If you're managing creative individuals, you understand that pouring lots of time into planning after a while doesn't continue reducing the unknowns. Generating a perfect plan of execution appears plausible and valuable but ends up being impossible. After an appropriate amount of time, we need to find as many ways as possible that don't work and rapidly arrive at the ways that do. Preproduction in our heads must give way to making, experimenting, failing, learning, and succeeding. Having your team running a localhost web server on their own computers and reviewing their work with handhelds delivers them more quickly to that ideal final "succeeding" step. It certainly ensures that customers never see the ugly middle parts of "experimenting" and "failing."

These are all key reasons to test your website on a phone or tablet typical of what your target audience will use to view your website. Our work only matters once it's seen correctly on devices.

PUT ALL YOUR DEVICES ON THE SAME WI-FI NETWORK

Can we make connecting our phone and tablet to our machine running Apache localhost as easy as possible? Yes, and a shared network helps that greatly. What do we mean by "shared"? That the development machine and phone can "talk" to each other. The phone is normally on a cell network run by one of the big national wireless carriers. Conversely, development computers are on a home or office network typically provided by private Wi-Fi.

Getting your work computer on a cell phone network where phones dial numbers is not helpful. Is the opposite direction a better choice? Yes, your phone can get onto a Wi-Fi network through its "settings" menu. Once there, it calls the computer through its IP address. If that term seems overly technical, please push that concern away. It's easily thought of as a number computers use to communicate to one another. We normally use a human-readable version of that such as `www.focalpress.com`, but in fact, that name is a synonym for a computer number called the IP address. We say the computer "resolves" that name into a number, allowing the convenient alias for human beings.

How does a computer resolve a human-readable name into an IP address? Domain Name System (DNS) servers store all known human-friendly names and the matching computer-readable addresses. As you can imagine, these are crucial parts of the Internet and must work reliably and quickly.

Once your phone is on the same Wi-Fi network as your computer, you're ready to get started. Same thing applies to your tablet. If it's on the Wi-Fi network, it's ready. If your computer is plugged into the wall with a network cable, that's fine. The cell phone can still talk to it "over the air," but the network must eventually all be shared in common. Ask your office network expert for confirmation if you're not 100% sure. One thing you can do is confirm that the phone's status bar shows a Wi-Fi connection icon rather than the cell phone network symbol. Also, if its web browser can reach out to common websites, that is a good indicator success is within your grasp.

Your next move is aiming your mobile browser at your work machine. Once a connection is made, Apache serves up your website in progress, and you'll see glorious triumph. Even so-called failures will be triumphs because they propel you one step closer to a final, workable solution.

GETTING STARTED CONNECTING PHONES AND TABLETS TO YOUR COMPUTER

Let's get to the good stuff. Let's get your phones and tablets talking to your personal Apache server. It is, after all, what we've been building toward. Many designers and developers will have thought this process full of complexity far beyond them and not an option for daily work. Believe me that it's possible.

Surely these doubts cause heartache, as creators intuitively feel checking on device is an imperative part of their work. Confirming our work in real-world conditions must feel like a final line item in any professional checklist. Now believe it when I claim this can be done at any time in the workflow. Ideally, it's so easily accomplished that you will want to do it as often as you come up with sufficiently changed HTML, CSS, and images. Reaching for devices ought to be easy, because most of us have a phone or tablet within reach.

CONNECTING A PHONE AND TABLET TO AN OS X MACHINE

We start by assuming your OS X–based machine is running Apache web server and attached to your network and that your tablet and phone are attached to the same network via Wi-Fi. Of course, we think of Wi-Fi simply because the mobile devices can't be hardwired into your LAN as your computer might.

After that step, the most important information is the unique identifier your computer has. It's assigned when your hardware connects to the local network and is called an IP address. Let's find out how to get that now:

1.   On your OS X–driven machine, open the "System Preferences" dialog box. This is available from several places, most notably the "Apple" icon.

2.   Click on the "Network" icon.

3.   You'll see an entry called "Status," which ought to report "Connected," as well as a message specifically telling what your computer "IP address" is. Make a note of this number, because it's exactly how your mobile devices will "call" the computer and talk to it. In turn, that tickles Apache web server to display your website files. Please realize this IP address will change from time to time as you attach to the network. It's a "dynamic" address, so don't be surprised when it changes.

4.   Pull a phone or tablet from your pants pocket, purse, or messenger bag. Launch your favorite mobile browser (for example, Safari or Chrome) and input the URL shown in your OS X network tab. For example, mine looked like this at one time: `http://192.168.0.217`

5.   As you've seen before on the desktop browser, your mobile browser will bring up whatever files and folders Apache finds in your working directory. If it's a list of folders, clicking on one of them will bring up its file contents or an index.html if present.

CONNECTING A PHONE AND TABLET TO A WINDOWS MACHINE

We begin assuming that your Windows-based machine is running Apache web server and attached to your network and that your tablet and phone are attached to the same network via Wi-Fi. Of course, we think of Wi-Fi simply because the mobile devices can't be hardwired into your LAN as your computer might.

After that step, the most important information is the unique identifier your development machine has. It's assigned when your machine connects to the local network and is called an IP address. Let's find out how to get that now:

1.   On your Windows-driven machine, open a Command Prompt window. Admittedly, this will look a little low level, but please have faith. There's only a little time spent here, and it's worth learning this specific task.

2.   Type the command `ipconfig` and skim the lines of information the computer responds with. One line will report something like "IPv4 Address . . . 192.168.0.247." Make a note of this number, because it's exactly how your mobile devices will "call" the computer and talk to it. In turn, that tickles Apache web

server to display your website files. Please realize this number will change from time to time as you attach to the network. It's a "dynamic" address, so don't be surprised when it changes.

```
Wireless LAN adapter Wireless Network Connection:

   Connection-specific DNS Suffix  . :
   Link-local IPv6 Address . . . . . : fe80::1dcb:4165:ef14:e07a%12
   IPv4 Address. . . . . . . . . . . : 192.168.0.247
   Subnet Mask . . . . . . . . . . . : 255.255.255.0
   Default Gateway . . . . . . . . . : 192.168.0.1

Ethernet adapter Local Area Connection:

   Media State . . . . . . . . . . . : Media disconnected
   Connection-specific DNS Suffix  . :

Tunnel adapter isatap.{94FD7623-951B-45FC-8E9C-B7430C4C2E83}:

   Media State . . . . . . . . . . . : Media disconnected
   Connection-specific DNS Suffix  . :

Tunnel adapter Local Area Connection* 11:
```

3. Pull a phone or tablet from your pants pocket, purse, or messenger bag. Launch your favorite mobile browser (for example, Safari or Chrome) and input the URL you read in the command prompt. For example, mine looked like this at one time: `http://192.168.0.247`

4. As you've seen before on the desktop browser, your mobile browser will bring up whatever files and folders Apache finds in your working directory. If it's a list of folders, clicking on one of them will bring up its file contents or an index.html if present.

You may find your mobile devices don't connect to your computer. When this happens, I check to see if it's because the Windows Firewall is running. As a protective measure benefitting you, the firewall stops connections to your computer. In this case, it's stopping connections that you actually want. Here's how you turn off the Windows Firewall.

1.   Click on the Start menu and select "Control Panel"

2.   The dialog box shows many configurations, and one of the last ones is called "Windows Firewall. Find it and click on it

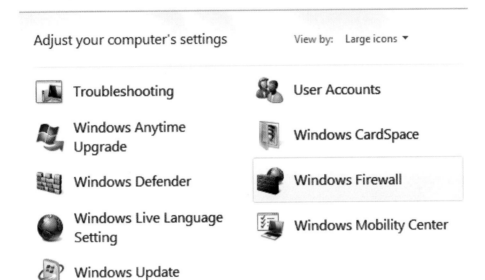

3.   On the side, look for an option called "Turn Windows Firewall on or off" and click it

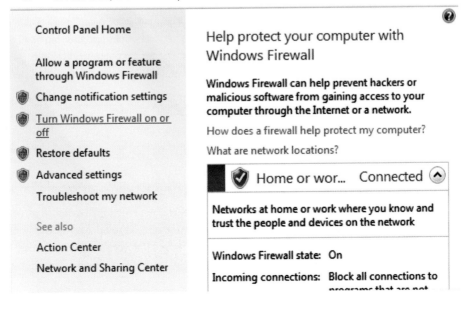

4.   The dialog box will show customization options. For the "Home or work network location settings," click "Turn off Windows Firewall" and press the "OK" button

Customize settings for each type of network

You can modify the firewall settings for each type of network location that you use.
What are network locations?

Home or work (private) network location settings

    ○ **Turn on Windows Firewall**

        ☐ Block all incoming connections, including those in the list of allowed programs

        ☑ Notify me when Windows Firewall blocks a new program

    ◉ **Turn off Windows Firewall (not recommended)**

Public network location settings

    ◉ **Turn on Windows Firewall**

[OK]   [Cancel]

5.   You've successfully turned off the Windows Firewall on your work computer, and Apache ought to receive requests from your devices and respond as expected. Feel free to turn Firewall back on when you're done testing.

GAINING CONFIDENCE THROUGH TESTING

At this point, you ought to be experimenting with your website work in progress on your mobile device. It is served up from your work computer thanks to Apache server. Why is this important? Now you can confirm your work, on at least your own phone, anytime you want to. No need to wait on a QA to become free and read their report of your updates. No need to wait to find bugs once they're on the production server and live for the entire world to see. This tool gives you the power to gain one of the most significant things we can achieve in modern web-based work: confidence. Confidence that:

- Your site works and appears on devices as expected
- You've polished your work, making it look great on device
- Bugs are found and fixed before your customers stumble across them

CONNECTING A DESKTOP MACHINE TO A DESKTOP MACHINE

One of the goals of this book is to enable you to better test your responsive design as you develop it into action. Ideally, when you're designing and coding, you're constantly testing on device or emulated devices. Why continuously testing? It proves that your work is a success. If it's not a success, then "quickly failing" means you get past the routine problems and glitches that strike all developers. We could take all the time in the world crafting the perfect plan but never know if it works while it's only in our design journals. Without actually making something, the entire time we're stuck in our own heads wondering as we leave out the people around us. Teammates, leaders, and clients won't see progress and constantly ask when will our work be ready. Continuously testing lets us gain confidence in our work and reassures everyone around us when we ask them to follow our lead and believe in our vision.

I still recall the day I told my QA teammate that she could browse to my development environment and manually test our latest build running on my desktop computer. The range of emotion on her face from confusion to surprise to understanding was fantastically fun to witness. She realized that when the shared test server was occupied by another teammate, she could still carry on running our latest work on my machine. Viewing it with her desktop browser hitting my own Apache server running on my development machine meant progressing on her testing tasks. No longer blocked, she could follow up by taking out her cell phone and testing it further on her handset. Her tasks went from "blocked" to "in progress," and her day became a lot better when I offered up this alternative option.

Testers can easily make use of connecting both devices and their desktop machines to a developer's work computer for confirming their team's work. Finding, documenting, and fixing bugs can happen well before work gets out to public-facing servers. All the time spent in this cycle means more polish for achieving higher-quality and more reliably functioning websites and web apps. Testing is of course not limited simply to QA experts. Anyone can participate in this activity, especially as code is submitted relatively late toward a deadline. "Code slams" happen when creative individuals push to gain as much time as possible to complete their work. Avoiding overload does mean managers, artists, and developers need to slip out of their comfort zones and slide into testing. Every annoying bug found means one less embarrassing one that customers might find.

LIMITATIONS

You might be wondering, especially if you're a QA–minded person, how many tablets and phones can attach to your development computer before it breaks—or maybe not exactly "breaks" but fails in some way from an overload of connections. I encourage you to find out! Give it a workout like a trainer makes their client sweat at a gym session.

As far as I know, there are no practical limitations for how many phones, tablets, and computers can hit your work machine. From my experience lining up a table of half a dozen phones and a few teammates from their laptops, I've never encountered a problem. That's the typical sweet spot of such a test, but your mileage may vary. Survey your site with a trusted set of handhelds representing your small, medium, and large-sized phones and tablets. Include the three most popular desktop web browsers as well. You will pull this tool into your content-creation workflow, testing legibility and presentation of your website rather than stress-testing network responses or server capacity.

Web servers are efficient due to their RESTful nature. REST is an acronym for representational state transfer, which describes a technology via which a browser requests data from a web server on behalf of a user action—for example, load the page from this URL. The browser sends over everything it can think of, giving the web server context for the request. The server listens to everything told to it as if it has never heard from that user's browser before. It replies as quickly as possible, the connection is closed, and the two forget about each other. This keeps life simple for servers and for browsers, but the user might feel a bit forgotten and lonely in that exchange if they knew better.

Perhaps now you're having an "ah-ha" moment because "cookies" popped into your head. You're thinking they're an important invention because they're one of the few ways servers can leave clues behind on a user's web browser. Cookies store small details servers use to remember past successful interactions for making better future ones.

No Network? No Problem!

When you've put into practice the tools covered in this chapter, I can guess you're convinced how useful attaching devices to your work computer is. Constantly viewing your work-in-progress website served up by Apache localhost is a sure way to see that your project is heading in the right direction. You might already have a problem in mind with the instructions for setting up the test environment. One of the most important conditions mentioned is "all sharing the same network is easiest," but what if you don't have a network?

What if your work laptop, test phones, and tablets can't share the same network because it doesn't exist, or at least doesn't exist as an open Wi-Fi easily accessed by your secondary laptop and mobile devices? Why would this ever happen? If your laptop was connected to a network, why wouldn't it be over Wi-Fi that your mobile devices can use as well? I've seen firsthand and heard stories from colleagues that clearly demonstrate this predicament.

Scenario one is having a job in client services and working a contract on site. Imagine when you have an extended stay in the client's office packed into a tight, sweaty corner meeting room. Making things even more challenging is that their overworked IT department only lets you have a network cable plugged into the Ethernet port cut into the wall. No login credentials for the wireless network are offered. That's a severe lack of Wi-Fi.

Scenario two starts when someone is United States–based with a service contract from a United States-based mobile phone carrier. When traveling to Europe with work, that person might sadly discover that roaming data-plan charges across the ocean are crazy expensive. Casually attaching a mobile device suddenly becomes as expensive as a fine dining experience in a star-rated restaurant. That's a severe lack of Wi-Fi.

Scenario three starts with employees of a top-secret government facility so paranoid that they do not allow any of their staff access to Wi-Fi. They have a dedicated hardwire from their laptop to the wall, and there's no open Wi-Fi to speak of. That's a severe lack of Wi-Fi.

Do you remember those stylish yellow Ethernet cables strewn along the floors that chair wheels were always bumping over? It's time to bust those out once again. In each of the scenarios mentioned, the design-and-development staff has a clever work-around. Modern laptops can reverse the stream of their Wi-Fi hardware when physically attached to a network. How? By creating a so-called ad hoc wireless hotspot that phones and tablets can ride along when attached to the laptop. From there, it's a matter of getting the hosting laptop's IP address and hitting it using the mobile browser. Then the laptop's localhost Apache will serve up the website exactly as you expect it to and exactly when you need an inventive fix.

> The phrase "ad hoc" is not technical jargon but in fact comes from Latin. Its meaning refers to anything that's spontaneously created for serving a particular need.

CREATING AN AD HOC WIRELESS HOTSPOT ON OS X

Establishing an ad hoc hotspot with your OS X–based laptop begins with a wired connection to the network. More than likely, this is an Ethernet cable snapped into a port cut into the wall. Just like old times!

1. Bring up the "System Preferences" dialog box, for example through the Apple pull-down menu

2. Click on the "Sharing" icon

3. Click on the checkbox entitled "Internet Sharing"

Computer Name: Ken's MacBook Air

Computers on your local network can access your computer at:
Kens-MacBook-Air.local   Edit...

On	Service
☐	Screen Sharing
☐	File Sharing
☐	Printer Sharing
☐	Remote Login
☐	Remote Management
☐	Remote Apple Events
☑	Internet Sharing
☐	Bluetooth Sharing

● Internet Sharing: On

Internet Sharing allows other computers to share your connection to the Internet. Computers connected to AC power won't sleep while Internet Sharing is turned on.

Share your connection from: Thunderbolt Ethernet ⌄

To computers using:

On	Ports
☐	Bluetooth PAN
☐	Thunderbolt Ethernet
☐	Thunderbolt Bridge
☑	Wi-Fi

Wi-Fi Options...

?

4.   Choose "Thunderbolt Ethernet" from the list titled "Share your connection from"

5.   Check the "On" checkbox for the "Port" called "Wi-Fi"

Your OS X laptop is now functioning as an ad hoc hotspot, a dedicated wireless network that shows up to mobile devices in a manner similar to that of any wireless router you've used before. When devices attach to the laptop's network (more on that in the next section), the mobile browser needs to use the laptop's IP address. You've looked up that number before, but as a refresher, follow these steps:

1.   Bring up the "System Preferences" dialog box, for example through the Apple pull-down menu

2.   Click on the "Network" icon

3.   Look for the Status: Connected message that tells what your laptop's IP address is. For example mine, shows `192.168.0.217`. Don't forget this is dynamic, so don't be surprised when it changes from time to time.

Location: Automatic

Thund...Ethernet
Connected

Status: **Connected**

Thunderbolt Ethernet is currently active and has the IP address 192.168.0.217.

Wi-Fi
No IP Address

Bluetooth PAN
Not Connected

Configure IPv4:   Using DHCP

Thund...lt Bridge
Not Connected

IP Address: 192.168.0.217

Subnet Mask: 255.255.255.0

Router: 192.168.0.1

DNS Server: 192.168.0.1

Search Domains:

Advanced...   ?

Assist me...   Revert   Apply

The laptop's IP address is what you type in your handheld's mobile browser to call up the Apache web server. From there, you view your pages and folders as you would normally.

CREATING AN AD HOC WIRELESS HOTSPOT ON WINDOWS

Establishing an ad hoc hotspot with your Windows-based laptop begins with a wired connection to the network. More than likely, this is an Ethernet cable snapped into a port cut into the wall. Just like old times!

1.   Click on the Start menu and click on the "Control Panel" icon

2.   When that dialog box shows, click on "Set up a new connection or network" under the "Change your networking settings" list

Control Panel Home

Manage wireless networks

Change adapter settings

Change advanced sharing settings

See also

HomeGroup

Internet Options

Windows Firewall

View your active networks ———————————— Connect or disconnect

Home network

Access type: Internet
HomeGroup: Joined
Connections: Local Area
                          Connection

Change your networking settings

Set up a new connection or network
Set up a wireless, broadband, dial-up, ad hoc, or VPN connection; or set up a router or access point.

Connect to a network
Connect or reconnect to a wireless, wired, dial-up, or VPN network connection.

Choose homegroup and sharing options
Access files and printers located on other network computers, or change sharing settings.

3.   A new dialog box titled "Choose a connection option" shows. Click on "Set up a wireless ad hoc network"

Choose a connection option

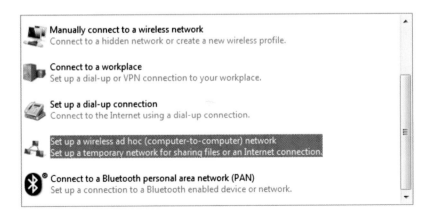

Manually connect to a wireless network
Connect to a hidden network or create a new wireless profile.

Connect to a workplace
Set up a dial-up or VPN connection to your workplace.

Set up a dial-up connection
Connect to the Internet using a dial-up connection.

Set up a wireless ad hoc (computer-to-computer) network
Set up a temporary network for sharing files or an Internet connection.

Connect to a Bluetooth personal area network (PAN)
Set up a connection to a Bluetooth enabled device or network.

Next   Cancel

4.   A new panel shows that explains what it means to "Set up a wireless ad hoc net-
      work." Read it for more details if you like. Press the "Next" button to advance to the
      next step.

5.   This is where you define the micro-sized, wireless, local-area network that your
      laptop emits. In the "Network name:" field, give it some easily remembered name
      such as KDawgLaptop. The easiest way to enable device connection is to choose
      "No authentication (Open)" from the "Security type" list, but of course anyone can
      connect to your laptop in that mode. Press the "Next" button when you're done
      with your configuration settings.

Give your network a name and choose security options

Network name:	KDawgLaptop|
Security type:	No authentication (Open) ▼ Help me choose
Security key:	☐ Hide characters

☐ Save this network

Next   Cancel

6.   You'll see one more panel in the dialog box. It reviews what you've created and encouragingly reports that your newly created network is ready to use.

The KDawgLaptop network is ready to use

This network will appear in the list of wireless networks and will stay active until everyone disconnects from it. Give the network name and security key (if any) to people you want to connect to this network.

Wireless network name: KDawgLaptop

Network security key: unsecured

To share files, open Network and Sharing Center in Control Panel and turn on file sharing.

Recommended options:

🛡 Turn on Internet connection sharing

Share an Internet connection on an ad hoc network

Close

Your Windows laptop is now functioning as an ad hoc hotspot, a super-tight wireless network that shows up to mobile devices in a manner similar to that of any wireless router that you've used before.

Experiment with this over time and learn more about how this feature adds value to your development toolbox. Leaving the ad hoc network "Open" is the easiest way for your phone and tablet to make a connection and browse your laptop. It's also the least secure, leaving it literally open for anyone in the surrounding area to gain access if they think to. In your office, this is probably no problem. In a coffee shop, in an airport, or on a client visit, this might be a risk you don't want to take.

When devices attach to the laptop's network (more on that in the next section), the mobile browser needs to use the laptop's IP address. You have looked up that number before, but as a refresher, follow these steps:

1.   Click on the Start menu and click on the Command Prompt icon

2.   When that program runs, type the `ipconfig` command to find out details about your network connection, a connection no doubt via hardwire into an Ethernet port in the office wall.

3.   Look for the grouped entry titled "Ethernet adapter Local Area Connection:" and scan its few lines for one reporting "IPv4 Address."

```
Ethernet adapter Local Area Connection:

   Connection-specific DNS Suffix  . :
   Link-local IPv6 Address . . . . . : fe80::59a2:be06:46a6:a885%11
   IPv4 Address. . . . . . . . . . . : 192.168.0.251
   Subnet Mask . . . . . . . . . . . : 255.255.255.0
   Default Gateway . . . . . . . . . : 192.168.0.1

Tunnel adapter isatap.{0CE0089C-4CB6-4513-8B00-9680BADBF46E}:

   Media State . . . . . . . . . . . : Media disconnected
   Connection-specific DNS Suffix  . :

Tunnel adapter Local Area Connection* 11:

   Connection-specific DNS Suffix  . :
   IPv6 Address. . . . . . . . . . . : 2001:0:9d38:6abd:342b:3546:b7bf:971c
   Link-local IPv6 Address . . . . . : fe80::342b:3546:b7bf:971c%18
   Default Gateway . . . . . . . . . : ::

Tunnel adapter isatap.{400863F8-5A28-4AC6-B5E9-A399F680DAB2}:
```

4.   Write down that number. For example, mine shows `192.168.0.251`. Don't forget this is a dynamic number, so don't be surprised when it changes from time to time.

The laptop's IP address is what you type in your handheld's mobile browser to call up the Apache web server. From there, you view your pages and folders as you would normally.

ATTACHING YOUR IOS DEVICE TO AN AD HOC WIRELESS HOTSPOT

Once you've turned your laptop into an ad hoc wireless network, you'll want to tap into its invisible power by attaching your handheld device to it.

For an iOS phone and tablet, begin with:

1.   Opening the "Settings" app

2.   Click on the "Wi-Fi" option

3.   Wait for the device to sniff the air around you and look for the network name you gave your laptop. Expect it to appear under the "Choose a Network" heading. There's a chance that your laptop network may show up under the heading "Devices."

    ❮ Settings   **Wi-Fi**

    Wi-Fi

    CHOOSE A NETWORK...

    Other...

    Ask to Join Networks

    Known networks will be joined automatically. If no known networks are available, you will have to manually select a network.

4.   Click the line item when it appears. You ought to attach to it automatically if it's "Open." If you gave it security settings, enter the password when prompted.

5.   When attaching to your Windows laptop, your phone may display a pop-up telling you that your laptop "Is Not Connected to the Internet," and you can confirm that is fine by pressing the "Join Anyway" button. It's not a problem, as you only need to get as far as the laptop and not beyond it to the public Internet.

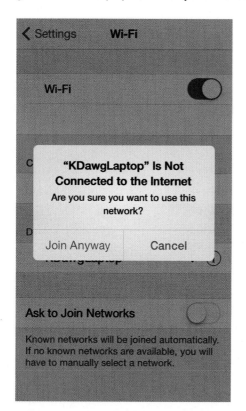

In the previous sections, "Creating an Ad Hoc Wireless Hotspot on OS X/Windows," you ought to have inspected the laptop to find and record its IP address. Hitting your work laptop and viewing its Apache localhost is now simple because all your hardware is now sharing the same network. Prove that out by opening your mobile browser, for example Safari, and type in the laptop's IP address in the top search input bar.

ATTACHING YOUR ANDROID DEVICE TO AN AD HOC WIRELESS HOTSPOT

Once your laptop is turned into an ad hoc wireless network, attaching your handheld device to it lets you tap into its invisible power.

For an Android phone and tablet, connecting to a Windows laptop appears to be unsupported at the time of writing this book.

To connect to an OS X–driven laptop, begin with:

1.   Open the "Settings" app

2. Click on the "Wi-Fi" option

3. Wait a moment while the device sniffs around and looks for the network name you gave your laptop. Once you see it listed, click on it, and you'll see a dialog box pop up to confirm the connection. If you gave your ad hoc network security settings, this is where you enter a password.

In the previous sections, "Creating an Ad Hoc Wireless Hotspot on OS X/Windows," you ought to have inspected the laptop to find and record its IP address. Hitting your work laptop and viewing its Apache localhost is now simple because all your hardware is now sharing the same network. Prove that out by opening your mobile browser, for example Chrome, and type in the laptop's IP address in the top search input bar.

Seeing What Your Users Will See

In my mind, the fantastic use of the Apache localhost serving up your website to your mobile device is that it represents what your customers will eventually see. You're viewing your work on phones, tablets, and computers just as they will. You'll see concretely if your work is going to meet their needs, at least physically. For example, are device-specific breaking points triggering as you think they will on the devices you test? Do resources such as stylesheets, JavaScript, and images get served up "over the air" without undue delay? Does the most useful information show top to bottom and left to right? Does it go another direction if your user's countries want it that way?

You've already experimented with Apache localhost serving up your website project while you work on it. Now you can attach to your personal development environment with a phone and tablet while walking around your office and be mobile just as your customers eventually will be. Try to feel the site as they eventually will feel it. Are they frustrated? Confused? Is something important off screen or shrunk too small? Do they feel empowered, satisfied, delighted, or relived they can find what they need using your site?

Concrete, firsthand impressions gained from you living the experience of your users are instructional in ways a personal template cannot match. Create a checklist of how you'll test your site, write it down in a document, and share it with your team as a testing strategy. Try using these real-world scenarios as jumping-off points for your experiments:

- On a phone walking into bright sunlight
- Distracted while surrounded by random conversations
- On an iOS phone and its browser; on an Android phone and its browser
- On a tablet held landscape then flipped around to portrait
- While walking around the office bumping into things
- Stuffed into a cramped waiting room chair, laptop teetering on crossed knees

All this work is in service of our customers. How can we have empathy for them? It's one of the most powerful words in our language, and it's popping up in talks and articles more often. Why? What problems are solved when we feel what our users feel? Feelings start by viewing and interacting with our websites, using customer devices in environments similar to theirs. It'll be amazing when you begin looking at your website as your users do and seeing that your first designs aren't what they need. Validating your assumptions through customer points of view will always synthesize another answer far better than your original. It's better because it's even more richly informed by the user experience.

Granted, we're still attached to our computers in an office, and we'll never draw a perfect picture of their lives given various physical limitations. But still, this is much better, don't you agree? It's more helpful that we admit we won't have all the answers at a project's kickoff and early design phase. Spending time to understand the challenges and problems and opportunities for a project is always crucial. Otherwise we waste time building things that don't matter. Even so, spending too much effort designing the perfect answer takes time away from building and discovering the final true details. Testing in this manner will help surface those valuable answers for your work.

Fail Fast, Iterate Quickly, Succeed More

What are some of the key understandings our teammates want to know as part of development and debugging?

- As an engineer, I must know, is the work functional, reliable, and simple?
- As an information architect, is your content seen when and where it needs to be?
- As a designer, you must ask, where does your work need polish?
- As a team leader, you're wondering, is my team performing to the level that they can? Do they have blockers? Do they have the toolbox necessary to help them deliver what's promised on time?

You've read much about the fail-fast mantra in startup culture. It's found throughout the Lean UX literature, and it encourages us to try building the smallest useful thing, see how real people respond when they use it, and then make little adjustments toward our original thinking to strive for a better outcome. It might seem laughable that old software projects took years to complete, but they did, and some still do. If we can iterate on a big problem by breaking it down into smaller ones, we're going to do better because we don't need to imagine as much before asking someone to build it.

Software—and I assert that websites are software and becoming more feature rich and app-like—are difficult to build. We ought not to impose more process and structure on a team in an attempt to reduce defects and problems. Ideally, our experienced and educated teams strive for building good work. Instead, we need to admit that bugs and errors will occur and use tools like the ones presented in this book to bounce back from mistakes with agility.

Take it from Tom DeMarco and Timothy Lister in their classic book *Peopleware*:

> *Fostering an atmosphere that doesn't allow for error simply makes people defensive. They don't try things that may turn out badly. You encourage this defensiveness when you try to systematize the process, when you impose rigid methodologies so that staff members are not allowed to make any of the key strategic decisions lest they make them incorrectly.*
>
> Tom DeMarco and Timothy Lister, *Peopleware: Productive Projects and Teams*, 2nd ed. (New York: Dorset House Publishing, 1999, p. 8)

These tools don't necessary make solving problems easier, but they will help you discover them sooner and allow you to get to the hard part of fixing glitches and bugs well before your real users do. Self-discovery is a valuable quality, but most practitioners don't expect to find it in their toolbox. This one amplifies that ability. Many bugs go out the door and into production because they were hidden from view. Seek them out often, and deliver higher-quality work with great professional discipline.

Virtual Hosts
Making Many Out of One

What Can Make Apache Web Server Better?

By now you've installed Apache on your personal development machine and conducted your first experiments in serving up your website to connected devices. As you've had a chance to see your work in progress on real-world handhelds, you've found breaking points in your responsive web design working. Images will scale up and down as needed to match changing screen widths. You've found that your stylesheets and JavaScript resources come across the air and land on your handhelds quickly enough to satisfy your impatient and busy customers.

You've taken up this powerful tool, internalized its value, and brought it into your design development workflow. I absolutely expect that by using it, you have made quality polish changes faster than ever before—changes based on more frequent critiques from your team-mates and demos to your clients because your work is more easily viewed in real-world conditions. Each of your milestones ought to deliver better-quality HTML, CSS, and JavaScript code, as bugs are more easily and more quickly found and fixed without dragging them on to subsequent milestones. You may find each milestone is functional, reliable, simple, and production ready.

I hope you have completely learned how to display your website through localhost for viewing on connected devices, played with the process, and gained confidence. With enough practice comes self-assurance of how the tools work. From there, I hope you've used your learning as an opportunity to serve your teammates by showing your experience with them. If you foster a team culture of sharing and learning, the result will be a good team getting better.

The next level of sharing is with the larger community. What community? It could be meeting up with your local professional group to compare notes. It could be speaking at a regional or national conference. It might be sending out an enlightening tweet, putting up a library into open source, or submitting a pull-request that fixes an existing source code repo. The form this next level of sharing takes is up to you, but it's worth it because it makes all of us better.

As you've gotten the hang of using Apache localhost well enough to teach your peers and share with the larger community, you must be wondering, "Is there something better?" Some people might think that's ridiculous. They think you ought to be satisfied and happy with the new tools you have now. It's only human nature to be discontented just as we reach a sufficient level of comfort and plenty. I think asking questions such as "Is there something better?" is how we're going to get to the next professional level of our craft.

In fact, this tool has a next level of "better." Granted, it's not crucial for getting your work done, but in fact, it's a next-level technique worth learning and experiencing firsthand. It's using Apache's notion of "virtual hosts."

Brief Introduction to Virtual Hosts

As you've been following along, you currently have one website hosted locally. It's proving a big help, but you probably have many projects going on at once. You have a new website in preproduction, continued support of a client site in production, a hobby project, and your company's own home site. I know this happens all the time because designers and developers tell me so when I'm out speaking at conferences.

I'm presenting virtual hosts to you as a way of keeping all those sites active on your development machine but separate enough to make sense of the projects individually. Virtual hosting is the feature of Apache web server that enables you to run many websites at the same time on the same machine.

How does a virtual server work? Practically speaking, it consists of individual bits you already know. When the parts are packaged up, they form into a powerful tool for your toolbox. Virtual servers simply incorporate:

- Your website's files organized in a folder
- A configuration file with specific details (another `.conf` file)
- Behind a site URL (`www.YourWebSite.local`)

Your website's folder is simply a collection of resources typically used to build up any site that you've ever made. It contains a bunch of `.html`, `.css`, `.js`, and `.jpg` files.

The configuration file is similar to the `.conf` file that you read and edited in Chapter 4 when setting up your server for "intermediate experience level" mode. We'll find out it's a different one that we'll introduce in the next section. You'll use it to tell Apache all your various website project folders.

An exciting part is naming the site with its own URL. It will connect to a folder on your local-host machine, but it looks and behaves more like the final product. There's surely a cool factor having a custom URL naming your virtual server. If that's not impressive enough, think of how convenient it is typing in a brief, descriptive, memorable URL as opposed to one constructed from localhost and various nested folders.

Creative leaders will appreciate this feature. Virtual hosts on your team's development environment are an effective way of retaining past sites. You can quickly verify that past sites are working and are ready to roll. Copies of current sites representing polished, functional milestones are always available for client demos that you show either when visiting their offices or on site in your own. Typing in a URL that's reminiscent of the final production site makes a compelling demo. We all know from reading storybooks as children that names have great power. This is a power we can wield in our working lives. Virtual host names bring an extra level of reality into your creative presentations and raise new opportunities for critiques and evaluation.

CONFIGURING A VIRTUAL HOST ON OS X

In Chapter 4, we set up Apache to serve pages from its default `htdocs` folder and modified its configuration to serve web pages from our own projects folder. These two steps are fine for many designers, artists, and developers. One more way Apache can better work for us is if we take advantage of its "virtual hosts" feature. This makes it look as though several websites are running from our single work computer.

Each virtual web server has its own name, for example, `http://www.tstringjs.local`, that when typed into your web browser comes back to your work machine instead of going off to search for an Internet site. Apache knows to serve up files from a folder that we tell it about.

1. Launch your favorite text editor for OS X (could be TextWrangler or another)

2. Click "File-> Open" to navigate to the folder Apache is installed in by default `/etc/apache2`

3. Open the file called `httpd.conf` with the text editor

4. Page down and look for the first line we change that looks like this one, which was line #499 for me:

```
# Virtual hosts
#Include /private/etc/apache2/extra/httpd-vhosts.conf
```

5. Remove the "#" character that starts the second line so that it looks like this:

```
# Virtual hosts
Include /private/etc/apache2/extra/httpd-vhosts.conf
```

The pound "#" character has special meaning that tells Apache to skip that line as if it's simply a comment for the human reader. For example, it could be a reminder telling why a choice was made. In this case turning off a feature until it's needed.

6.   When you first type, a dialog box might pop up that asks you, "Are you sure you want to unlock 'httpd.conf'?" because it's a special file. Press the "Unlock" button as confirmation that you know what's happening.

7.   Save the file. A dialog box might pop up that asks you, ". . .wants to make changes. Type your password to allow this." Do so and click the "Allow" button.

8.   Click "File-> Open" and navigate to the folder Apache is installed in by default `/etc/apache2`

9.   Click on the `extra` folder inside it

10.   Open the file called `httpd-vhosts.conf`

11.   Delete everything that you find in this file. For me, that was about 40 lines referring to an example "Virtual Host" that's not important.

12.   Type this block of text to setup your overall project site. Make it match the working projects folder you used in the previous section. It tells Apache where our general working folder is:

```
<VirtualHost *:80>
    ServerName localhost
    DocumentRoot "/Users/ken/trees"

    <Directory "/Users/ken/trees">
        Options Indexes FollowSymLinks
        AllowOverride All
        Order allow,deny
        Allow from all
    </Directory>
</VirtualHost>
```

13. After that block, type this, telling Apache to establish a named virtual server, one that may be opened in a web browser with `http://www.tstringjs.local`. All files will come from a particular working folder that holds everything that makes up the website.

```
<VirtualHost *:80>
    ServerName www.tstringjs.local
    ServerAlias tstringjs.local *.tstringjs.local
    DocumentRoot "/Users/ken/trees/tstringjs"

    <Directory "/Users/ken/trees/tstringjs">
        Options Indexes FollowSymLinks
        AllowOverride All
        Order allow,deny
        Allow from all
    </Directory>
</VirtualHost>
```

14. Save the file and close it

15. Click "File-> Open" and choose a special file called `hosts` from the special location `/etc`.

16. Add this line at the bottom of the file matching the same "server alias" that you added in the `httpd-vhosts.conf` file a few steps back:

```
127.0.0.1 www.tstringjs.local
```

17. Save the file and quit your text editor because we're done with the changes. A dialog box might pop up that asks you, ". . .wants to make changes. Type your password to allow this." Do so and click the "Allow" button.

18. Restart Apache by opening a Terminal window and entering `sudo apachectl restart`

19. Open your web browser and enter `http://www.tstringjs.local` into the search bar. Your website's working files are displayed and rendered as if it were its own server.

Now you have a locally running web server that mimics multiple web servers, with each one delivering a folder of source code matched with a site name. That's right, multiple servers from a single machine. Quickly confirming what you've already guessed, you may easily add multiple "VirtualHost" definitions in `httpd-vhosts.conf`.

Operating systems reserve a "hosts file" for you and me to use to tell it extra information. Specifically, we use it to declare a network-connected server (a host) that's not found under normal circumstances (DNS lookups). We can add a line in the `hosts` file that pairs a human-readable server name with an IP address. Because this file is uniquely important to the O/S, it's given special read/write permission that usually takes administrative privilege.

Don't forget how we added matching entries in the `hosts` file. You'll do that for each virtual host you tell Apache to serve.

CONFIGURING A VIRTUAL HOST ON WINDOWS

In Chapter 4, we set up Apache, served pages from its default `htdocs` folder and modified its configuration to serve web pages from our own projects folder. These two steps are fine for many designers, artists, and developers. One more way Apache can better work for us is if we take advantage of its "virtual hosts" feature. This makes it look as though several websites are running from our single work computer.

Each virtual web server has its own name, for example, `www.tstringjs.local`, that when typed into your web browser comes back to your development environment instead of searching out on the Internet. Apache knows to serve up the files from a folder that we tell it to use.

1. Open on File Explorer and click on the folder you installed Apache in, for example, `C:\Apache2.2` if you entered that following the installing section

2. Double-click into the `conf` folder

3. Open the file called `httpd.conf` with a text editor of your choice (could be Notepad or another one)

Organize ▾ Include in library ▾ Share with ▾ Burn New folder			⊞ ▾ ☐ ❔
★ Favorites	Name	Date modified	Type	Size
	📁 extra	4/2/2014 7:25 PM	File folder	
📚 Libraries	📁 original	4/2/2014 7:25 PM	File folder	
	charset.conv	4/2/2014 7:25 PM	CONV File	2 KB
👪 Homegroup	httpd.conf	4/2/2014 7:25 PM	Text Document	18 KB
	magic	4/2/2014 7:25 PM	File	14 KB
🖳 Computer	mime.types	4/2/2014 7:25 PM	TYPES File	54 KB
💾 Local Disk (C:)				
💾 Local Disk (D:)				
🖧 Network				

6 items

4.   Page down and look for the first line we change that looks like this one, which was line #478 for me:

```
# Virtual hosts
#Include /private/etc/apache2/extra/httpd-vhosts.conf
```

5.   Remove the "#" character that starts the second line so that it looks like this:

```
# Virtual hosts
Include /private/etc/apache2/extra/httpd-vhosts.conf
```

> The pound "#" character has special meaning that tells Apache to skip that line as if it's simply a comment for the human reader. For example, it could be a reminder telling why a choice was made. In this case turning off a feature until it's needed.

6.   Save the file and close it

7.   Return to the Explorer folder

8.   Double-click into the `conf\extra` folder

9.   Open the file called `httpd-vhosts.conf` with a text editor of your choice (could be Notepad or another one listed later)

10.   Delete everything that you find in this file. For me, that was about 40 lines referring to an example "Virtual Host" that we don't need.

11.   Type this block of text to setup your overall project site. Make it match the working project folder you used in the previous section. It tells Apache where our general working folder is:

```
<VirtualHost *:80>
   ServerName localhost
   DocumentRoot "d:/trees"

   <Directory "d:/trees">
      Options Indexes FollowSymLinks
      AllowOverride All
      Order allow,deny
      Allow from all
   </Directory>
</VirtualHost>
```

12.   After that block, type this, telling Apache to establish a named virtual server, one that may be opened in a web browser with `www.tstringjs.local`. All files will come from a particular working folder that holds everything that makes up the website.

```
<VirtualHost *:80>
   ServerName www.tstringjs.local
   ServerAlias tstringjs.local *.tstringjs.local
   DocumentRoot "d:/trees/tstringjs"

   <Directory "d:/trees/tstringjs">
      Options Indexes FollowSymLinks
      AllowOverride All
      Order allow,deny
      Allow from all
   </Directory>
</VirtualHost>
```

13.   Save the file and exit your editor. It needs to be restarted in the next step.

14.   Run your text editor with special permission. We'll edit a file unique to the operating system that requires administrator privilege. Click on the "Start" menu and right click on your editor's icon and select "Run as administrator" from the pop-up menu

15.   Press the "Yes" button if Windows shows a pop-up dialog box confirming the special action asking "Do you want to allow the following program to make changes to this computer?"

16. Open a file called `hosts` that exists in this special location:

    `c:\Windows\System32\drivers\etc`

17. Add this line at the bottom of the file matching the same "server alias" that you added in the `httpd-vhosts.conf` file a few steps back:

```
127.0.0.1 www.tstringjs.local
```

18. Save the file and quit your text editor because we're done with the changes

19. Restart Apache

20. Open your web browser and enter `www.tstringjs.local` into the search bar. Your website's working files are displayed and rendered as if it were its own server.

TString.JS

Example of translated text strings and foreign language support

Read the technical article on my blog

Fork me on GitHub

[English ▼] [Select]

Imaginary Network Program Listing

Title: Underwater Sea Adventure   **Date:** Sep 6th 2015, 2:00 pm   **Channel:** National One
Synopsis: As one person is nearly captured the other one thinks no way she will let that happen.

Title: Stories Of Neverwhere: Prince Amazing   **Date:** Sep 7th 2015, 2:45 pm   **Channel:** National Three
Synopsis: Prince Amazing must return home and discovers he has lost the magic belt of pants holding +1.

Title: Slightly Amazing Together   **Date:** Sep 8th 2015, 2:45 pm   **Channel:** Reruns Again!
Synopsis: A fairly okay group of semi-skilled individuals come together to save Neverwhere.

Title: Dull Brain   **Date:** Sep 9th 2015, 12:30 pm   **Channel:** The Ocho
Synopsis: Dull Brain defeats one villain only to reveal a new nemesis from an unlikely source.

Now you have a locally running web server that mimics multiple web servers, with each one delivering a folder of source code matched to a name. That's right, multiple servers from a single machine. Quickly confirming what you've already guessed, you may easily add multiple "VirtualHost" definitions in `httpd-vhosts.conf`.

Operating systems reserve a "host" file for you and me to use to tell it extra information. Specifically, we use it to declare a network-connected server (a host) that's not found under normal circumstances (DNS lookups). We can add a line in the `hosts` file that pairs a human-readable server name with an IP Address. Because this file is uniquely important to the O/S, it's given special read/write permission that usually takes administrative privilege.

Don't forget how we added matching entries in the `hosts` file. You'll do that for each virtual host you tell Apache to serve.

ADVANCED APPLICATION OF APACHE

As you've followed along with this tutorial, you've graduated to the next level of Apache web server usage. Running a server locally makes you more productive. Polish comes more quickly, bugs are found sooner, and viewing your work in progress on real-world handheld devices is casually accomplished. Besides being cool, virtual host names let you demo your work in a way that looks nearly complete.

Virtual host configurations can keep consistency among all of the developers on your team. For example, every artist and developer knows they're creating `http://www.coolsite.local`. Each and every person on the team could jump on a teammate's machine, open a browser window, and bring up that site's standard `.local` virtual hostname to see the latest and greatest. The files, however, can be located in any folder on any development machine. Everyone can have a bit of personality in where they work (`DocumentRoot`), but it's given the same name by a standard decision (`ServerName/ServerAlias`). This is the subtle, advanced power of virtual hosts.

Hosting companies sometimes offer virtual hosts for running several customers' websites on the same physical computer server. Some people might think that's sketchy, because each customer would want their own dedicated hardware. True enough, and some will demand that and will also pay extra for the privilege. Dedicated resources are always an upsell and are certainly necessary for some applications. Others will figure out they have websites that are simply not used enough to generate the customer traffic to justify an extra expense.

Other levels of hosting support include virtualization at the server machine level rather than the web server. Establishing more privacy and protection is the customer offering in this case.

Each physical server hardware runs software that emulates a self-contained operating system with Apache running inside it. This boxes off different customers' work from one another while remaining shared on the same hardware. This is more common with cloud-based hosting services.

Internal operations teams may come to the same conclusion when hosting their company's own sites on their own network. If a handful of low-use websites can be served up as virtual hosts from the same Apache web server, that's a good use of a shared environment. It's a cost-cutting measure that helps a budget last longer as new websites are being spun up and launched. Collect websites coming to end of life on a shared box as usage naturally winds down. Wisely choosing how to use limited resources is a key skill for all of us to learn and practice. Virtual hosts are an advanced tool that empowers that decision.

LIFE IS NOT A HAPPY PATH

As a software engineer, I love the "happy path." I search for it, I build along it, and I test using it as a reliable roadmap. If you've never heard the term, the "happy path" is an optimized workflow I use while moving through a website or app that shows the least resistance. Happy paths don't have crashes, and they produce the most positive results for each step taken. As one small success follows another, it allows me to reach a successful conclusion as quickly as possible to see the features I'm building. Do you recognize that navigation pattern in your own work? You probably instinctively do the same at times purely because it's quicker and makes development of a workflow faster and easier.

As my favorite QA expert, Cindy, jokingly reminds me, "Life is not a happy path, Ken."

In fact, her hilarious cautionary tale informs our decisions during the development process. I can't help but think that if we only build software and websites according to how we quickly blast through them, we're missing all the sidetracked turns our real users take. Those turns can become infrequent but crucial dead ends that produce bugs, display necessary refinements, or conclude in unexplained conditions that assume too much unrevealed context.

Happy-path development strikes at the heart of how difficult designing, coding, and building a website is. Historically, the tools for viewing, testing, and debugging our sites have been obscure. I aim to empower you to put all these essential tools easily within your reach so you can practice and gain skill. Apache web server and its virtual hosts feature are next-level tools for you to bring into your workflow. They allow you to make mistakes, find them before others see them, and fix them as quickly as possible.

We ought not to stress out trying to decide all the best answers in preproduction. It's impossible to expect that we can sit down and brain-sweat out all the details by thinking and planning on a whiteboard or paper prototype. That's okay. Realize those activities are crucial, but then get on with the task of fabricating a project. Start building and forming up your site from the base ingredients of artwork and code. Then test it innocently, childlike, without preconceived notions, just as your new users will. Tools such as localhost and attaching mobile devices give us license to fail quickly, recover immediately, and stay in the creative flow more often. Creative leaders ought to empower their teams to take risks in order to discover much-needed answers.

President of Pixar Animation Ed Catmull writes in his book, *Creativity, Inc.*,

> *In a fear-based, failure-averse culture, people will consciously or unconsciously avoid risk. They will seek instead to repeat something safe that's been good enough in the past. Their work will be derivative, not innovative. But if you can foster a positive understanding of failure, the opposite will happen.*
> Ed Catmull with Amy Wallace, *Creativity, Inc.: Overcoming the Unseen Forces That Stand in the Way of True Inspiration* (New York: Random House, 2014, p. 111)

Life is not a happy path, but it's far from a miserable one, too. Map your roads in exhaustive detail and ensure all the dots are connected by lines forming both the expected and surprising paths your customers need to best use your technology.

Drifting DocumentRoot Up Into the Cloud

Chatting one day with my buddy, Young, a phenomenally talented, adventurous, and technically minded designer, I was struck by an incredibly useful technique that I want to share with you. It's an advanced notion that you can mix into this already advanced topic of virtual servers. Really, this technique could just as easily help designers and developers at the intermediate level of web server use.

We've already reviewed that `DocumentRoot` in the Apache config files lets you refer to a website project by the team's standard name (`www.TheNewHotness.local`) while storing your project files wherever you want to on your personal computer. This small creative freedom offers a fine choice to you for best organizing your universe however it most makes sense to you. What if there's a better place to store your website files than your personal machine? "Better" might be subjective, but here's an alternative you could find interesting.

If you use a cloud-based file-storage service such as Google Drive or Dropbox, you might have installed their sync application on your computer. Both of these services in particular offer extensions for Windows and OS X that make their server-based folders appear as if they actually exist locally. What happens if you point your Apache configuration file's `DocumentRoot` to the folder established by the cloud service? That sounds intriguing, doesn't it?

Why should you consider this crazy way of `DocumentRoot` at all? Why does it matter whether we can store files online if we simply have our development machine with us all the time? Laptops are portable enough, and that seems to work for us so far. Of course, this scheme isn't for everyone, but thinking it through, we can figure out several cool and valuable reasons for placing our website's work files on a cloud storage service:

- You can edit your files on any computer that's connected to the Internet. Maybe you're off site visiting a customer and want to make a tweak before a presentation and only your teammate has their machine. Perhaps you have a desktop machine at work that doesn't move but want to make adjustments on your computer when you get home.

- Many cloud-based file services offer automatic backups. Extra protection offers a reassuring guarantee that's a tremendous benefit for smaller groups that might not have on-site duplication facilities.

- If website files are stored in a publically shared folder, you can preview your work to other people, including clients and teammates in other cities, states, or countries.

- Some companies lock down their corporate networks with virtual private networks (VPNs) to protect their resources. While I'd never tell you to break your company's intellectual property rules, I can tell you that putting files on a cloud-based file server can let you work more flexibly if you need to. Use your best judgment under these conditions.

If you go off and try out this trick now, you'll probably find that it fails. Most of the problem revolves around a permission issue. The cloud-service application extends the operating system and owns the right to read and write files to its folders. Permissions are kept private and "need to know," so to speak. Apache doesn't need to know and is kept from peeking into the folders. A work-around is easily within grasp: We can change the permission levels of the folder to ensure all applications across your machine can easily access it.

CHANGING FOLDER PERMISSIONS ON OS X

1. Open a Finder window and navigate to the folder created by your cloud file server that you want to set as a `DocumentRoot`

2. Right click on the folder and select "Get Info" from the pop-up menu

3. Look for the label called "Sharing & Permissions:" and click on it to open it if it's closed

4.   On the entry named "everyone," select the Privilege `Read & Write`

Hardcore OS X users getting more confident with this seemingly "low-level" stuff might have fun skipping Finder and instead dropping into a Terminal window, changing to that folder path, and issuing `sudo chmod-R 747 folder-name`. Don't be a sad panda if you're not ready for this—it's all a matter of practice before perfection.

A Real Web Server in Your Backpack

Do you feel as though you've learned everything you can possibly know about Apache web server? You ought to, because there's relatively little remaining that we haven't gone over together. There are many tools for you to discover in the remainder of this book, but Apache localhost is surely one of the strongest and most worthy ones for you to study. Adding this tool to your workflow has made your professional work more organized, brought a more final look to your progress, and helped you find issues across a range of viewing devices.

It's not overstating to say that you now have a true material competitive advantage sitting on your work computer. As you learn more, getting smarter at your craft with additional tools in your creative workflow, how will you approach what you've learned? Will you hold on to your knowledge, keeping it as an edge? Will you share your learning, looking to raise the level all around you? Improving teammates means they have a better foundation to learn upon and share what they master, improving you in turn.

You've worked through Apache web server from beginning to end, and there's little remaining that you might need to know. There are surely more things to learn about it, but pursue them when you have a concrete need. Whatever those details are, be confident that you have the foundation to jump from and leap across the knowledge gap to understanding.

Are you amazed that you have tucked under your arm the same sort of web server that can run a company's public image? It's absolutely true. Did you ever think you'd get to that point? Well, you have.

CHAPTER 7

Get Together on GitHub

Introduction

Where can you get the most freshly brewed code for your favorite library, framework, or tool? We all know about the various homepages hosting these time-saving tools, but what about the VIPs? Where do they go? Isn't there somewhere extra special—an amazing place all the cool kids hang out? Where they pass among themselves the latest and greatest updates to their finest creations?

No, of course not—that's absurd to think. There's no special, amazing, exclusive club for the elite open-source creators to join forces and dominate the world. It's all publically available to everyone on GitHub. If you've never heard of GitHub, then you're in for the start of a fun journey in which you can quickly lose yourself. Even if you do know of this social coding site, there are details and tips found in this chapter for using it in ways you might not have expected.

GitHub is a valuable place to easily access the source code for the most current developer tools. One of the commonly used libraries for front-end web development is jQuery. You know it as well as I do because it's a de facto standard in our industry. We have visited its friendly and informative homepage for updates and instructions. Clearly found in the page's upper right-hand corner is a download link. Everyone is only one click away from getting this incredibly helpful library.

When you download jQuery from their web site, you're getting its source code in final form, efficiently compiled and ready for production. It's a great service for all of us. Many other libraries, tools, and frameworks follow this model. Another way exists. When you download jQuery from GitHub, you're getting the raw, uncompressed source code.

Many of your favorite tools are hosted on GitHub. Visiting that site, you can download the complete source code in active development by the programmers dedicated to improving

most every tool that strikes your interest. Access to knowledge like this can be incredibly powerful. Reading through the original source code to any project offers insights such as:

- How to organize a complicated work
- What logic exactly triggers in any function you use
- Best practices for generally developing algorithms

The value doesn't stop here. Some of the most useful source code you could take advantage of doesn't have a well-polished landing page as you've come to expect. Plenty of work
is housed on GitHub for public consumption and only mentioned by its author in a modest
fashion, perhaps announced by a tweet or brief article on a blog. Understanding how to find
these rare gems on a social-focused source code host like GitHub is a sure way for you to
power up and rise above your competition.

> The Git in GitHub is the name of a particular type of revision control system (RCS) that
> makes up a client/server system for storing the source code that makes up a project.

Let's go look around on GitHub for tools that can become obvious advantages for you.
We'll pull down a few tools, review reasons software engineers have flocked to GitHub, and
examine ways to access GitHub. Try them and find out which becomes an outstanding addition to your creative toolbox.

Tool: Responsive Design Testing

One of the key ways responsive web design is totally different than anything else is that it must
show a single page in many ways. Media query rules in the selector styles held within a CSS file
shift your markup HTML around, potentially dramatically, based on the screen size of the reader.
You need to think of your overall content but pour it into each of the device form factors you're
choosing to support. Keeping all of the images of this site at once in your head is tough to say the
least. It is especially tough to keep straight as the minor stuff gets tweaked and polished over time.

Author Matt Kersley has created Responsive Design Testing, a fantastic tool that helps you
see the big picture of your website. It unpacks your responsive design as a series of interactive
snapshots, framed side by side, at each of the major screen sizes. Having an overview like this
is a great way to compare and contrast how your work flows and breaks according to your
style rules in context with one another.

Look at the project here:

```
https://github.com/mattkersley/Responsive-Design-Testing
```

Browse the project's page on GitHub. It's worth taking a moment to examine the major sections on the page:

- A list of all the source files that make up the tool's project
- A pane subtitled README.markdown that documents an introduction and description of the project (you'll notice this filename and presentation style is a convention among authors)
- A "Download ZIP" button
- A "Clone in Desktop" button
- An input labeled "HTTPS clone URL"

This is the web interface to GitHub, and you'll come to recognize it. Projects hosted here will have the same homepage layout. Once you learn to navigate GitHub for one project, you've learned it for every other.

Introductory Way of Using GitHub

Your browser becomes your access point into GitHub via its web interface. As you look around the previously mentioned project, you can click on any of the files held within it to see its contents. Read through the code; select it to copy and paste for use through your text editor. This is useful if you want to quickly take a peek at a particular file and all right for this project because it's made up of a few files.

What if a project has many more files and folders contained within it? Don't inspect them one at a time. Look for the button labeled "Download ZIP" and push it. Receive the project files sorted into folders bundled up in a single, compressed archive exactly as you expect it ought to behave. Uncompress and expand the .zip file on your computer and view it in your browser to see what it can do. The next page shows a quick example of what the testing tool looks like on my machine viewing a site that I've built.

My point here is to briefly introduce this useful project to you. Give it some time and decide if you want to incorporate it into your power toolbox of success. You might find that it's a solid tool for quickly gaining an overall impression of how your website work is progressing across the device sizes you're targeting. Using it can help you answer sanity-check questions such as: Are breaking points clicking in with the CSS media query rules? Are fluid images properly scaling within their parent containers? How does the shape of content compare among a handful of viewing sizes?

Play with the project you've downloaded and consider whether you should make changes to it. You have the complete source code sitting on your machine, after all. What are some interesting ways to change it? I have some ideas:

- Add another viewport size that matches a device you want to support
- Have it default to your site's URL
- Tweak the colors to match your typical tools and make it feel more familiar

240 x 320 (small phone)

320 x 480 (iPhone)

768 x 1024 (iPad - Portrait)

480 x 640 (small tablet)

1024 x 768 (iPad - Landscape)

None of these tweaks feels useful enough to suggest back to the project's owner. At the same time, they're incredibly helpful to you, well worth your time to investigate, and easily possible.

More importantly, this is a fine jumping-off point into GitHub. Just think of how many creative authors inventing projects are hosting them publically on this socially driven site.

WHY DO SOFTWARE ENGINEERS LIKE GITHUB?

If you've already heard about GitHub and know a bit about it, you'll know it's popular with software engineers and programmers. You might be wondering why that is. I'll take a pass at explaining why I think it's a great place to house my code:

- The fact that GitHub is functional, reliable, and cloud based means I can get to it and my project code everywhere I want.
- It's based on Git, a fundamentally unique and exciting way of controlling source code revisions within a team (or even an individual).
- Social interaction has a place: I can star (like), watch (follow), and fork (share) projects.
- Collaboration tools make it easy to invite fellow creators into a project.
- You can open up the development process with wiki (documentation), issues (bugs and regressions), and pull requests (fixes and improvements).
- It can be made private when I need to keep special projects close to me.

Revision control systems are crucial for allowing a team or even an individual to track changes to files over time. If we can go back through the history of a file, we can tell when a bug was introduced and more clearly identify the change and revert it out to get working again. We can see which teammates are contributing to a project and how. We can mark the repository with a tag when a significant event occurs, for example an important release. That gives us an archival-quality bookmark we can return to or a note for what to test that will soon go out the door for public use.

> The terms "project," "source code," "codebase," "repo," and "repository" all seem interchangeable. Which is the right word to use here? In fact, they can all be right depending on the listener and from what era she started her career.

It seems obvious professional builders would want source control, right? This didn't always happen, of course. Lots of projects happen without it at all. Scary dangerous! Some teams simply exchanged code by copying their latest files to a floppy disk and handing it over. That was called "sneaker net," and we laugh at it now. Having a copy of working project source code on another computer, like a server, is incredibly valuable—especially when the server is routinely backed up automatically.

Git does one better, and everyone on the team with the project is a server. It's what's known as a distributed system, and it is one of the fundamental ways Git is a novel invention. It also means that for a solo worker, there is a way to have a Git project on your work computer, commit changes to it, and have a revision history to go back to for safety's sake, even without it being on a remote server. Check that out one day when you want to learn a pro tip.

Hiring practices have changed since GitHub was spun up into the public. I've seen GitHub involvement viewed as a supplement when candidates are considered for job openings. So much of programming is the code written, and companies want to see what the prospective teammate's code looks like. Open-source technology is key to most companies' technology stack, and seeing a candidate's contribution to the community makes an impression on interviewers. Some will debate if a GitHub account and commit history will replace the resume.

I'm intrigued by GitHub's financial model. My simple understanding of it is that they'll let us host projects on their site for free, but they're public and open to everyone. Public projects are open for reading, but permission to write to them is strictly controlled by their owners. If we want private repos that are hidden and invitation only, we can subscribe and pay based on the number needed. That's what I do, if you're wondering. I have a monthly subscription that allows me a small number of private projects that I want. I have more public projects than private ones. One of the public projects holds all the source code examples in this book. Give it a look, clone the repo, play with it, and share the link.

```
https://github.com/KDawg/ResponsiveWebDesignToolkit
```

Intermediate Way of Using Git (and GitHub)

If the introductory way of using GitHub is through its web interface, then what's the next step? I'll say it's downloading a stand-alone application that has full support for the Git command flow. We'll keep it simple as to what Git commands we use now to get you started.

Of course, software engineers traditionally work in the plain-text, command-line world more than anyone. Chapter 11 reviews that state of mind, tradition, and purpose. Git began its life as a command-line tool, and many companies have sprung up that produce excellent applications with full graphical user interfaces (GUIs) matching your expectations of a modern program. Here is a list of some of them. Check them out and pull down a few to give them a test run to see which is best for you:

- GitHub for Mac, GitHub for Windows
- SourceTree (for Mac and Windows)
- SmartGit (for Mac and Windows)
- Tower (for Mac only)

To start with, I'll simply recommend that you download and install GitHub's program (also called a client). It's free, fully functional, and well documented. Once you download and install the GitHub client, you must sign up with GitHub to download source code from a project you're interested in using. In the Git world, this means you will "clone" a project, which makes a copy on your work computer.

When you look at a GitHub project on its web page, as we did earlier, you'll notice a button called "Clone in Desktop" that's suddenly very interesting to us. Click it and notice that it calls up your GitHub client app and confirms with you before it pulls down a complete copy of the project's code. Now you have a duplicate of it with which to play to your heart's content. Don't be concerned if you make changes to the files now stored on your computer. Anything you do is kept local and private. You can't mess up the original author's work because she keeps control of it as the owner and maintainer. If you ever make changes that completely break your local copy, remember that you can always delete it and start over. Make a new folder and again clone the original project repository.

> Project code by nature is collaborative. It takes a few people with distinct skills to properly build it. GitHub introduces a social interface through its project web pages that offers watch (follow), star (like), fork (share), and pull requests for approval (write permission).

As an introduction to GitHub, you might have downloaded the ZIP file for a repo. With this client app, you will have access to many new features. Two of them are immediately worth learning:

- View history to see what users have made file changes in the past
- Synch (Git calls this a `pull`) to download all the files changed since the last time you did this or since the first time you cloned the project repository

There are many more Git commands that this client app exposes you to, but resist using them until you want to make changes and submit them back to the project owner(s). The next section gets into more detail on the Git workflow, but it becomes complicated quickly. Don't look into it until you're ready to take on some training time. I encourage you to do it, but wait for an opportunity to open up in your schedule and you can devote dedicated brain sweat to it.

There's an interactive tutorial where you can learn the basics:

```
https://try.github.io
```

A Git client like the GitHub application mentioned here is a great tool. Because it exists on its own, we can call it a stand-alone app. It stands on its own as a tool dedicated to this sole purpose. You might wonder if Git support can be built into another tool, and yes it can. For example, a more complicated and fully featured way to edit code is called an integrated development environment (IDE), and it's worth pointing out several well-known ones on the various operating systems that support Git access:

- Visual Studio (Microsoft)
- XCode (Apple)
- WebStorm (JetBrains)
- Eclipse

If this doesn't mean much to you now, then no problem, but in the future, it might be a good thing for you to look out for while you're building websites.

Advanced Way of Using Git (and GitHub) Command Line

When Git was first created, all its tools were command line only. This is a classic interface for programmers, and many still prefer using Git that way. Several Git apps that offer friendly graphical user interfaces are listed in this chapter and are highly recommended for your use. What follows here is a chance to catch a glimpse of what some of the command-line tools look like given a few commonplace workflows.

When you're curious to learn more about Git revision control, use the following descriptions for context and background in your research. Don't think that you need to learn how to use the command line immediately. It's not at all productive for you, and honestly I rely on my IDE of choice for its semi–GUI based access to Git commands. This is mostly a demonstration to satisfy your curiosity.

DOWNLOAD A PROJECT FOR THE FIRST TIME BY CLONING IT.

1. From a web browser, navigate to the URL for this book's GitHub project:

```
https://github.com/KDawg/ResponsiveWebDesignToolkit
```

2. Look on the page and see all the facts and stats that are common for any project hosted on GitHub. Look for an entry field with the label "HTTPS clone URL." You'll see a button beside it with a clipboard icon. Click this, and the project's clone link is copied to the system clipboard. We'll use this to download a copy of the project source code.

3. From the command line, change directory into the folder where you keep your projects. For my example, it's `cd trees`

4.   Enter this command to download a copy of the project: `git clone https://` `github.com/KDawg/ResponsiveWebDesignToolkit.git`

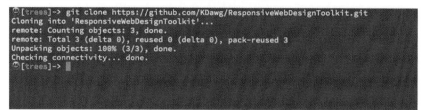

UPDATE A PREVIOUSLY CLONED PROJECT TO GUARANTEE ALL THE LATEST AND GREATEST IS AVAILABLE:

1.   From the command line, change directory into the folder where the project's files are stored from a prior Git clone

2.   Enter this command to download the latest and greatest version all of the changes made since you last updated: `git pull`

3.   You'll see real-time stats from Git as it collects all changes, compares your local copy with the origin server, and brings across all differences. If no new changes are available, it simply reports "Already up-to-date."

CREATING A NEW FILE

What do I do to create a file and upload it to the project? This is mentioned in the chapter and left as a bit of a future assignment for you to research when it's important. That's because this chapter aims to help you find, get, and use projects. Steps you find here are easily adapted to your Git client app of choice.

1.   From the command line, change directory into the folder where the project's files are stored from a prior Git clone and where you've edited a file

2.   Add the changed file that tells Git what you will send up: `git add README.md`

3.   Commit the changed file(s) with this: `git commit-m "add the landing page URL"`, which stores the changed files in a complete copy of the project repo stored on your computer

4.   Upload the files to the remote server with this: `git push origin master`, which takes all the files previously committed from your local server up to the origin master that sits on GitHub and refers to a branch of the code, which is by default the master branch

```
[ResponsiveWebDesignToolkit]-> git add README.md
[ResponsiveWebDesignToolkit]-> git commit -m "add the landing page intro"
[master 99dedf7] add the landing page intro
 1 file changed, 2 insertions(+)
 create mode 100644 README.md
[ResponsiveWebDesignToolkit]-> git push origin master
Counting objects: 3, done.
Delta compression using up to 4 threads.
Compressing objects: 100% (2/2), done.
Writing objects: 100% (3/3), 401 bytes | 0 bytes/s, done.
Total 3 (delta 0), reused 0 (delta 0)
To https://github.com/KDawg/ResponsiveWebDesignToolkit.git
   b31ea4d..99dedf7  master -> master
[ResponsiveWebDesignToolkit]->
```

MAKING CHANGES TO A PUBLIC PROJECT

What if I change a file by fixing a bug or tweaking it with enhancements? Get completely current with the project, branch from master, make changes, and then upload it for eventual approval with a pull request.

1. From the command line, change directory into the folder where the project's files are stored from a prior Git clone

2. Get completely current with all the most recent changes: `git pull`

3. Make a branch from the default branch, called master, that will contain all your changes wrapped with a bow: `git checkout-b my-helpful-change`

4. Edit various files

5. Add the changed file by telling git what you will send up: `git add README.md`

6. Commit the changed file(s) with this: `git commit-m "added more detail on the booga booga"`, which in fact stores the changed files in a complete copy of the project repo stored on your computer

7. Push the files up to the remote server with this: `git push origin my-helpful-change`, which takes all the files previously committed from your local server up to the original GitHub server, but this time in a particular branch of code.

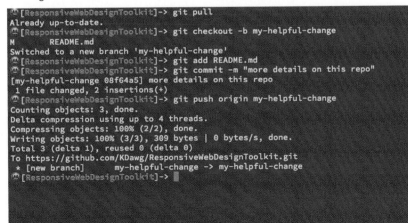

```
[ResponsiveWebDesignToolkit]-> git pull
Already up-to-date.
[ResponsiveWebDesignToolkit]-> git checkout -b my-helpful-change
M        README.md
Switched to a new branch 'my-helpful-change'
[ResponsiveWebDesignToolkit]-> git add README.md
[ResponsiveWebDesignToolkit]-> git commit -m "more details on this repo"
[my-helpful-change 08f64a5] more details on this repo
 1 file changed, 2 insertions(+)
[ResponsiveWebDesignToolkit]-> git push origin my-helpful-change
Counting objects: 3, done.
Delta compression using up to 4 threads.
Compressing objects: 100% (2/2), done.
Writing objects: 100% (3/3), 309 bytes | 0 bytes/s, done.
Total 3 (delta 1), reused 0 (delta 0)
To https://github.com/KDawg/ResponsiveWebDesignToolkit.git
 * [new branch]      my-helpful-change -> my-helpful-change
[ResponsiveWebDesignToolkit]->
```

8. Here's a collaborative bit. On the project's webpage interface, you can click on the "branches" tab and see the branch you've just pushed up to the project repo. Click on the "New pull request" button to announce to the project maintainer that you have changes you want her to review and merge with into master branch. If she approves of the changes and merges the pull quest, you've just made the world a better place!

This process is incredibly useful when working on a project that you own with your team. It's worth going through the professional discipline of merging any changes to the project via a pull request.

A pull request is the perfect place to do a code review. A code review is when one engineer reviews another engineer's changes, double-checking that changes are all good to go. I recommend putting multiple people on a pull request. For example, assign a new hire or someone unfamiliar with the feature, giving them a chance to look around and learn more.

Tool: Responsizer.JS

Here's another tool that you can pull down from GitHub by cloning a copy of it. If you drop Responsizer.JS into your webpage, you'll see it drawing the browser's reported width of your website in pixels. It's useful real-time feedback to you while reviewing your layout and testing the CSS rules.

```
https://github.com/KDawg/Responsizer.js
```

Certainly several desktop browsers have developer tools built in that report the window's dimensions in pixels. Does that make this a bit obsolete? Maybe on desktop browsers. However, the browser developer tools usually aren't available while testing on real mobile hardware. Seeing this little JavaScript report to you the exact width of the screen is a win for establishing and reviewing breaking points in your media queries.

Download it and drop it into your locally hosted website project and give it a go. It needs jQuery to work properly. Here's a brief example of how you'd add it at the bottom of your `index.html`—just like any other script file.

```
<script src="code/Responsizer.js"
    type="text/javascript"></script>
```

You'll see it respond quickly as it draws a centered box top aligned to your website as viewed in a browser. It changes color as it detects the width hitting one of the commonly accepted device breaking points. Here are a few examples of what it looks like.

e for the spelling test. St|the spelling test. Study |elling test. Study hard, g
and see you next week!|see you next week!| week!

What if you don't want that flash of color when it detects one of its predetermined boundaries? Change it. Page through the code and shut it down. What if you have another device width in mind and you want to add it? That change is even easier to do as you read the code. The power is yours while the source code is on your machine. Make it your own and personalize it.

Showing this to you is meant to inspire ideas in your head about tooling. If something doesn't exist and you could benefit from its existence, spend a little time and make it. Pull in a buddy and pair up on it to make the work go faster and catch more ideas to make it better. Browser tools are surely huge efforts put on by companies with great teams and budgets, but you and I can knock out little tools like these in an afternoon. Fine-tuning it from time to time is great fun. When you show it off to colleagues at work or at a meetup, you'll gain inspiration for bolting on new features.

Building tools may seem inconvenient, but as you use them, you'll feel happier and more productive. Automation is a goal I'm always on the look out for. If I do something routinely, I want to craft a little tool that removes the tedium of doing the task, especially if it's a task that leads to outcomes that help me put quality features and updates into the hands of my customers.

When you make something fantastic and useful, no matter how small, consider offering it up to the open-source community. Publishing it on GitHub is a perfectly fine idea.

Creating a New Project on GitHub

There are many tutorials on the Internet for using Git and GitHub. I'm not here to explain how to use them in detail but, rather, why you'd want to. These are high-level steps for making a repo and filling it with your code.

- Log in to `github.com`.
- Create a new repo.
- Clone it on your local machine using your Git client app.
- Create and write various source files using your code editor or IDE of choice.
- Add the files using your Git client.
- Commit the files.
- Push your committed files using your Git client.

The instructions change a bit based on which tool you eventually choose, but the fundamental idea remains the same.

Practice this on a side project to become smart and confident. It's worth the time, and it's nice to take an opportunity to learn on a low-stress hobby project. Then, when the time comes to perform in front of a group, you'll have real experience to guide your actions.

As you make changes locally to your project's files, you'll want to:

- Add each of the changed files in your Git client app
- Commit all of them (happens at once) using your Git client
- Push the changes in your Git client

Seems like I only told you to go to the GitHub website once, and that was to first create the project. The remainder is done on your workstation while you're in the daily grind of your creative workflow.

Another reason you'll navigate around the GitHub web interface is if you ever need to delete a project. You'll find detailed instructions on how to remove a project on their website.

Tool: Git

You know what would be a fun source code to clone and look at? The code for Git itself. Can we get Git? You already know the answer. Yes! Here's a link to the GitHub project page:

```
https://github.com/git/git
```

Feel free to open it up in your web browser and have a look around. From the project's description, I gather this is only a mirror. Mirrors are known to be copies that are reflected from an originating source hosted on some other server. I'm not exactly sure where that other server is, the more active master one, but that's all right. The point here is just to have a bit of a laugh while looking around at it.

Cloning a copy of this is done as easily as any other lesson that you've taken on in this chapter. What's the point of having all of this source code? I'm not exactly sure, but it's fun knowing we can do it. It looks as though most of the source is written in the system-level C programming language. That's even less instructive for you, but that's how it goes on the Internet. There is lots of code, lots of languages, lots of thoughts and points of view. Would we have it any other way? No! For surely diversity breeds strength and success.

JUST LOOK AROUND

There's so much code in the open-source world, how can you connect with something interesting? How can you discover a truly new idea to dig into? You can start by browsing GitHub Explore:

```
https://github.com/explore
```

There you'll find collections of code projects on display and organized around subjects GitHub curators want to bubble up to the surface. You'll find some of the most popular projects grouped by region, entertaining subjects, utilities, and anything else under the sun. It's worth spending time there just to see what's new, and what's new to you.

EVER ONWARD

We've had fun going through some smaller tools so far. Each is clearly meant to arrive at a particular outcome and solve a problem for its users. What about the really amazing, famous, super-popular libraries, frameworks, and tools? Do those exist out on GitHub? Can you see exactly what's under the hood of your favorite open-source project? Yes! To serve as inspiration and tempt your curious mind, here are links to some of the biggies hosted out on GitHub:

```
BackboneJS - https://github.com/jashkenas/backbone
Bootstrap - https://github.com/twbs/bootstrap
Compass - https://github.com/Compass/compass
Font Awesome - https://github.com/FortAwesome/Font-Awesome
jQuery - https://github.com/jquery/jquery
Modernizr - https://github.com/Modernizr/Modernizr
MomentJS - https://github.com/moment/moment
NodeJS - https://github.com/joyent/node
PhantomJS - https://github.com/ariya/phantomjs
Sass - https://github.com/sass/sass
```

Take your time and look around each of them. See what goes into all of them, their organization, their algorithms, their data structures, and the people who pour their time into them. Watch the subtle changes as live development progresses.

Have a look at the Issues section of each project. You'll see public discussions of which bugs are fixed first and which pull requests are accepted as the latest changes.

Most of these tools have well-maintained landing pages that keep up to date with deliverables. Can you get more current work from these GitHub project sites? Generally yes, but is it worth it? Maybe not for the big ones, but surely for the smaller tools that don't have well-produced landing pages. That said, even the big projects have fun insights to look at on the project page:

- If you know there's a bug you want stomped, you can at least read through the discussions going on in the Issues page.
- Keep an eye on the wiki pages, because they might have more details from the developers than what's on the project stand-alone landing pages.

- Have fun looking at pull requests to see activity happening as community members suggest changes to the owning maintainers.

One day, when you're ready, join in on any or all of those sections. Report a bug and a way to reproduce it. Even better, submit a fix to a bug. Even a small one such as documentation is welcome by these tireless project committers, because I believe many of them work on open-source projects in their spare time. Quality help is always welcome.

ALTERNATIVES TO GITHUB

By now you know that GitHub meets my daily professional needs. I use it, and so too do many of my colleagues and most of the open-source projects I use. There are enough alternatives that we have a real choice in the matter of hosting projects. Don't be confused, however, if open-source tools you are curious about are missing from GitHub. They might be found on an alternative, competing open-source hosting service such as:

- Bitbucket
- Project Locker
- CodePlex
- CloudForge
- Assembla
- SourceForge

Each source-code hosting provider has a different set of features. Some focus on public source-code hosting, while others specialize in private source-code hosting, and most support both. Some focus on Git, others on Subversion, and so forth. Some even provide enterprise editions if you have big company needs.

You and your team might be happy with any of these. Try out a few. You owe it to yourselves to make a well-informed decision. Please don't pick one in the mad rush as a project starts just to mark a checkbox done on a task list. Due diligence is your friend, and picking the tool that's the best fit with your team will amplify your skills in the best way possible.

> Does Git have alternatives? Yes. The basic idea of a revision control system that helps teams purposefully manage their source code has existed for decades. Alternatives include Subversion, CVS, Mercurial, and other proprietary systems.

Read Now and Write Out Something One Day

A common theme in this book is empowering artists, designers, and developers to examine and reach for the tools historically kept in the domain of software engineers. Source control and Git and GitHub are further examples of this. Look into them and use them well. Search for the open-source tools you use and think of how source control can help you if you're not yet using it.

In Chapter 2, I called for you to share a useful library with the world. Here's a place that your work, big or small, can live. It's social coding, and people will find it. To help folks discover your work, write about it. No need to formally invest in time-consuming promotion, but tweet, post on Facebook, and write a blog article. Get it out there and see what amazing things will happen. Help push forward the state of the art with a cool little hack. Don't hold back your good ideas, thinking it's all been done before by super-intelligent beings who drop genius from their fingertips onto their keyboards every morning over a cup of coffee.

Surely coffee is involved, but remember that some overworked creative person just like yourself started every incredible piece of software that you use daily. If you don't think much of your lovingly handcrafted artisanal code, someone else might think it's fantastic and exactly what they need at the right time. Put it out there, and it might become the next big thing! Even if you're only solving a simple problem, I believe the world continues to need needle, thread, and an awesome pattern printed on cotton more than it needs silk couture.

When you do write code to share, consider that you're an author, and an author's job is to communicate effectively. I think that means writing with an intent in mind and clearly guiding the reader toward it. When we communicate, we ought to convey meaning.

Robert C. Martin reminds us in his book:

> As systems become more complex, they take more and more time for a developer to understand, and there is an ever greater opportunity for a misunderstanding. There, code should clearly express the intent of its author. The clearer the author can make the code, the less time others will have to spend understanding it. This will reduce defects and shrink the cost of maintenance.
> Robert C. Martin, *Clean Code: A Handbook of Agile Software Craftsmanship*
> (Boston: Pearson Education Inc., 2009, p. 175)

Although his meaning might be in the context of a large body of source code written by many people over a long time, we can still draw inspiration from it. Even a relatively small amount of code ought to be written well. Taking the time to be clear benefits ourselves and the community we're serving. Also ensure that when shipping something out, you don't accidentally let slip private information—for example, a secret client code or application programming interface (API) key that you and your company signed up for.

I want to fill your core imagination with all the encouragement possible to build that custom piece of software. Take time to explore GitHub. See if someone else has scratched the same itch you have and already made the thing you were about to start cobbling together. If it's out there already, then use what's made. If it's nearly what you want, clone the repo and make some tweaks to it to fit your purpose. Once you're sure the code is functional, reliable, and simple, reach out to the original author and tell them the good news of your improvements. Perhaps they'd like to work with you to pull in your changes and formalize them inside their project.

Open-source technology is often built out in the open. It could start private, but at some point, it must be opened to the public. I believe once a project becomes sufficiently popular, the requests for bug fixes, optimizations, and feature enhancements come rolling in to the owner at a steady flow. If these projects are conducted during night hours and over the weekends, they're going to want help. Desiring help means engaging in a public collaboration process, and that generally winds up in a place like GitHub. Seeing the development occur could give you additional context when revisions and updates appear on the project's formal product landing webpage.

Contribute to your favorite projects. It could be very simple to start. Report a bug with a snippet of code that casually proves the point. Offer a fix to a bug. Sometimes that's as simple as a change to the documentation. If you see another user like yourself report a blocker in the Issues page and you know a workaround, offer it up to them. At least it could help them make progress while the programmers make final corrections. If you're a designer and the tool's creators are all engineers, offer them some firsthand context for how you use their tool and suggest changes they might not have considered. They might be happy and encouraged to hear from you, and your ideas could become industry best practices.

CHAPTER 8

Google Chrome

Browsing a Page and Reading Its Code

When Is a Browser More Than a Browser?

The web browser has turned into something very special. It may have begun life modestly as a way for users to view webpages, but it has evolved over time into something more. It's become a crucial tool for developing and debugging the very pages it views.

Whenever you're reading a page, you can easily open up the developer tools and have a look at exactly how it's made. If it's a page from someone else, we gain inspiration, pro tips, and jumping-off points. If it's your own page you can find out what's not quite right, be it a JPG, HTML, CSS, or JavaScript.

We can practice the most modern technique of designing in browser. By inspecting elements and changing them, we'll interactively add markup and style to instantly see what's up.

All modern web browsers provide sophisticated developer tools. I'll be covering Google Chrome because it's the most popular cross-platform web browser.

How to Develop for Mobile Without Devices in Hand

Chapters in this book have helped you connect your phone and tablets to your development machine to better test your responsive web designs. Now this chapter is telling you that you don't need to do that. "What's up?" you may be asking yourself. "Has Ken lost his mind?" I assure you, I haven't. It's simply a matter of admitting that handhelds are sometimes hard to come by. Even without the device, you can still take some steps to test against an emulation of it without ruining a day of productive work.

OPENING CHROME'S DEVELOPER TOOLS

Using a debugger is a great way to investigate buggy source code. The debugger's job is to show you what source code is running. The problem for authors is that a browser executes our code fast, and based on user interactions, we never know exactly where it is. Fortunately, you can tell a debugger exactly what line it should pause on using a breakpoint.

Imagine if an auto mechanic could freeze time and roll underneath a car while it's driving at full speed down the highway. That's what happens when the debugger breaks on a line of code. With the engine still running, we can inspect the underlying system as it works. For us, it's seeing the following:

- Inspecting the JavaScript as it executes and the data it holds
- Viewing HTML layout that forms the document's page
- Listing files requested and brought across from the web server
- Identifying all styles applied to every document object model (DOM) element

A feature-rich browser like Chrome allows you to crack open a webpage and look inside to see how it's working or find out why it isn't working. Given those tools, you have a better chance at seeing the logic that doesn't add up, styles that don't look good, or missing elements that leave holes in your page.

Opening the developer tools is simple enough. Take a moment to do it and look around a bit, briefly, before we dig deeply into specific features.

1. Run Google Chrome web browser
2. Click on the "View" drop-down menu
3. Select "Developer" submenu item
4. Select "Developer Tools" menu item

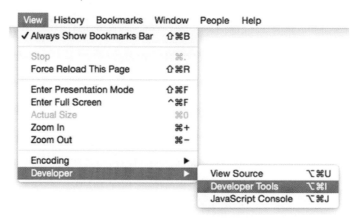

If this is your first introduction to the developer tools, you'll enjoy learning about them and working them into your creative workflow. Investing time in learning this tool will serve you well in terms of more easily finding and fixing bugs and quirks in your website work. Work includes HTML layout and structure, CSS appearance and inheritance, and even JavaScript if you're writing logic and rules. If at this point you're only writing one or two of those languages, you may find your confidence growing as your experience builds.

MOBILE EMULATION TOOLS

Because this book is about responsive web development, we'll have a look at the mobile emulation tool. You can clearly run this on desktop and resize your window back and forth to see how your design reacts to smaller and wider windows. It's more interesting to see how we can emulate the mobile devices we know are in the possession of our target audience. That audience is made up of nearly everybody at this point. Unfortunately, we can't possibly have all the phones and tablets that our collective audience will have, but yet we want and need to judge our work's quality before it lands in their world.

Chrome's mobile emulation toolset offers:

- Screen size—quickset by device name, but also free to resize
- User agent spoofing—lets the browser more accurately imitate the mobile device by telling the web server what it wants to know
- Bonus—not necessary but interesting for various applications: touch events, connection speed slow-down, geolocation overrides, gyroscope emulation

TOUCH EVENTS

In the Chrome emulation shelf, you can turn on the "Emulate touch screen" function by ticking the associated checkbox found under the "Emulation" tab. What does this do? Immediately we notice the browser's classic mouse pointer turns into a different shape. It's more of a round bullet. That shape tells where the hotspot is as you touch your website. It's round like a fingertip, and it's the diameter of a typical touch zone a person presents each time they tap a touchscreen.

You'll find certain touch events are now emulated by Chrome that will tickle whatever JavaScript logic you have associated with the following touch-specific events: touchstart, touchend, and touchmove.

| Console | Search | Emulation | Rendering |

Device   ☑ Emulate touch screen
Screen ✓   ☐ Emulate geolocation coordinates
User Agent ✓   Lat = [   ] , Lon = [   ]
Sensors ✓   ☐ Emulate position unavailable
                ☐ Accelerometer
                α: [0]
                β: [0]
                γ: [0]
                     Reset

Chrome's touch event emulation is easily tested with the following webpage. It's a concise demo that exercises the immediately useful touch-specific events for making interactions.

```html
<!DOCTYPE html>

<html>
<head lang="en">
  <title>Touch Events Test</title>
  <meta name="viewport"

    content="width=device-width, initial-scale=1.0">
</head>

<body>
<h3 id="touch-me-zone" style="background-color: lavender; padding:
50px;">Touch Events Test</h3>

<script type="application/javascript">
  var zoneEl = document.getElementById('touch-me-zone');

    zoneEl.addEventListener('touchstart', function() {
      console.log('touch start');
    }, false);

    zoneEl.addEventListener('touchend', function() {
      console.log('touch end');
    }, false);

    zoneEl.addEventListener('touchmove', function() {
      console.log('touch move');
    }, false);
</script>

</body>
```

When you copy that code over to a new page in your favorite text editor, or IDE, and view it in a browser, you'll see text printed out as you click and drop around the light-purple-colored box. You'll see the text, through `console.log()`, by opening the developer tools and clicking on the "console" tab.

You'll see that I choose using `console.log()` as a dependable debugging aid. If you're wondering why, it's because it comes from a technique I learned long ago when simply printing out text was the primary debugging tactic. Of course, there are many more inspection tools available in modern developer tools, and the JavaScript source-code debugger in Chrome is as good as any I've used in my long career. Still, I choose `console.log()` as a quick way to dump out information to see if some logic is triggered. It's especially useful when events happen many times a second and I want to see real-time data flowing into place.

Working code running on real devices wins arguments. Sometimes we don't have real hardware within reach. Mobile emulation tools let us stay productive and motivated as we design, build, and critique our work.

USER AGENT

In the Chrome emulation shelf, turn on the "Spoof user agent" function by ticking the associated checkbox found under the "Emulation" tab. Choose one of the predefined entries and then hit your website, either local or, more likely, an existing one on the Internet. Several dozen options are offered to you, but the most interesting ones are named after mobile devices. This is a device pretender to use while you're developing responsive web designs.

| Console | Search | Emulation | Rendering |

Device   ☑ Spoof user agent

Screen   ┌─────────────────────────────┐
              │ Android 4.0.2 — Galaxy Nexus ⬍ │
User Agent ✓ └─────────────────────────────┘

              ┌──┐
Sensors   │ Mozilla/5.0 (Linux; U; Android 4.0.2; en–us; Galaxy Nexus Build/IC │
              └──┘

"User agent" refers to the web browser working on your (the user's) behalf (as an agent). It's a series of letters and numbers and a few punctuation marks strung together that tell a web server a little bit about your setup—details such as:

- CPU architecture

- Operating system and version

- Your browser's name

- Compatibility with legacy browsers

Here's one example of a user agent string:

```
User-Agent:Mozilla/5.0 (iPhone; CPU iPhone OS 8_0 like Mac OS X)
AppleWebKit/600.1.3 (KHTML, like Gecko) Version/8.0 Mobile/12A4345d
Safari/600.1.4
```

Why does this matter? For the most part, it matters very little between websites in these days of modern web design. Historically, servers have "sniffed" user agents and offered up customized experiences such as:

- Warn about incompatibilities with a given browser

- Serve up different files such as a stylesheet

- Offer to download various add-ins like plugins or extensions available for your browser

- Redirect you to a completely different website based on a version built especially for a mobile device

You know those websites that redirect you from a desktop site to a mobile site? Building a completely custom website based on a mobile experience is a legacy idea held over from the days when mobile devices didn't have the power to render a well-designed website. This architectural choice already smells obsolete.

Today, we'd much rather build a single, fantastic site that's responsive and works well for laptops, tablets, and phones. If you're stuck with the architecture that redirects mobile devices to a specific website, at least you can use your desktop browser to test some of that when using a handheld device isn't practical.

NETWORK TOOL—WATCHING WHAT FILES GO ACROSS

Much of the slowness in a browser experience happens as files are transferred from a web server to the browser. Bigger files are slower, but sending lots of little files slows down the user experience, too. It might seem counterintuitive, but software engineers sometimes prefer a few bigger files to many smaller ones. Why is that? Lots of time is lost as the browser gains an initial connection to the web server to request the file. This is called latency.

You've probably judged this number-of-requests versus size-of-requests tradeoff before. Consider work you've done as a technically minded designer building websites in the past:

- Delivering a single sprite instead of multiple images
- Delivering a scalable icon font instead of dozens of static icon images
- Using Sass or Less to combine multiple stylesheets into a single one
- Concatenating several JavaScript files into a single one

These techniques can provide a noticeable speed boost and improve user experience. Please use more of them! It's good stuff.

Back to the idea of how relatively slow it is for the initial connection (latency), we can map out the steps and see how much slower it is on a cell phone:

- Energize the cell radio chip
- Negotiate a connection with the local cell phone tower
- Look up the web server's IP address from a name
- Connect to the web server and request a file
- Open a stream and bring the file across to your cell phone provider's internal network
- Download the file from the service provider to your phone

That seems like a lot of work, and it happens relatively fast, but it's far slower than what you see when on Wi-Fi. What's to do here? Use your browser's developer tool and click on the "Network" tab to see what files are pulled across the network from a web server to your local web browser.

Name	Met...	St...	Type	Initiator	Size	Time	Timeline
www.annaspellingwords.com	GET	200	text/html	Other	1.9 KB	137 ms	
AnnaSpellingWords.css?v=1.2	GET	200	text/css	www.annaspellingwords.com	3.5 KB	223 ms	
Analytics.js	GET	200	application/x-javascript	www.annaspellingwords.com	758 B	232 ms	
AnnaSpellingWords.js?v=1.5	GET	200	application/x-javascript	www.annaspellingwords.com	6.1 KB	224 ms	
jquery.min.js	GET	200	text/javascript	www.annaspellingwords.com	29.1 KB	91 ms	
correct.m4a	GET	206	application/octet-stream	www.annaspellingwords.com	29.7 KB	411 ms	
wrong.m4a	GET	206	application/octet-stream	www.annaspellingwords.com	31.8 KB	395 ms	
complete.m4a	GET	206	application/octet-stream	www.annaspellingwords.com	35.6 KB	493 ms	230 ms
ga.js	GET	200	text/javascript	Analytics.js:11			
master.json	GET	200	application/json	jquery.js:7845			
jquery.min.map	GET	200	application/json	www.annaspellingwords.com			
_utm.gif?utmwv=5.5.3&utms=1&utmn...	GET	200	image/gif	ga.js:63			
whats.m4a	GET	206	application/octet-stream	Other	23.6 KB	262 ms	
heres.m4a	GET	206	application/octet-stream	Other	17.4 KB	274 ms	
im.m4a	GET	206	application/octet-stream	Other	17.1 KB	340 ms	
doesnt.m4a	GET	206	application/octet-stream	Other	13.3 KB	318 ms	
dont.m4a	GET	206	application/octet-stream	Other	16.6 KB	255 ms	
isnt.m4a	GET	206	application/octet-stream	Other	14.6 KB	335 ms	
theres.m4a	GET	206	application/octet-stream	Other	15.1 KB	137 ms	
thats.m4a	GET	206	application/octet-stream	Other	16.8 KB	342 ms	
hes.m4a	GET	206	application/octet-stream	Other	18.1 KB	242 ms	
shes.m4a	GET	206	application/octet-stream	Other	22.5 KB	295 ms	
jquery.js	GET	200	text/javascript	Other	70.5 KB	160 ms	

Blocking 118.074 ms
Sending 0.120 ms
Waiting 145.020 ms
Receiving 229.943 ms

23 requests | 466 KB transferred

Remember that opening the developer tools is simply a matter of:

- Clicking on the "View" toolbar item
- Clicking on the "Developer" menu item
- Clicking on the "Developer Tools" submenu item

In this picture, you'll see each of the files requested, its size, and how long it took for the request to complete. Click on the columns to see the list sorted in different ways to help you interpret it.

Sorting by name alphabetizes the list so you can better see what files are sent. Sorting by type reminds you what category of files are sent.

Sorting the network file list by size is interesting as you focus on the biggest files. Ensure they need to be sent, which is probably the case, or figure out if they can be sent in a smaller form. For example, you might turn a .PNG image into a compressed .JPG if the image's transparency channel isn't used. Open-source tools exist to shrink the size of PNG files, "crushing" them, by removing unnecessary additional data.

Sorting the network file list by time is interesting as you focus on reducing how long it takes files to download to your reader. For example, working with one of your team's engineers, see if there are ways to store files on the user's browser (cache control). Another way of sending files more quickly is by uploading them to high-speed content delivery networks (CDNs) such as Amazon S3. Both topics are outside the scope of this book, but I've mentioned them to get you thinking and talking to your team.

Looking at the network graph might evoke feelings of confusion, helplessness, and anger, but please don't lose hope. It's another tool that you can bring into your workflow as you build your website. Use it as a gauge for how your website is performing as your team builds it. Software engineers realize the first step of reducing how long something takes is measuring and recording that time. Later changes can be timed, recorded, and judged better depending on which direction the timings go.

WHERE ARE YOU REALLY? LATITUDE AND LONGITUDE

Do you have a web app or website that depends on your user's current location? For example, letting them search around where they are right now for a thing they need most in life—like a coffee shop, movie theater, or grocery store? It's a natural, given mobile devices have built-in tracking hardware and our ever-increasing goal of making solutions personalized. What JavaScript logic lets us ask the user's spot in the world? There's a function called `navigator.geolocation()` that returns the user's latitude and longitude.

It's fine if you're testing this function on device in your comfy office chair, but you might be wondering: Will your code work for a customer in a far-off city? Even testing against a state nearby is interesting after a while. If you know the latitude and longitude of a city—you can easily look that up on your favorite web search site—use Google Chrome developer's tools to test. When you open the developer tools and switch on the mobile emulation feature, you'll see the "Sensors" option and the "Emulate geolocation coordinates" setting. Simply click on the checkbox to activate the feature and type in your test "Lat" and "Lon" values.

Console	Search	Emulation	Rendering

Device	☐ Emulate touch screen
Screen	☑ Emulate geolocation coordinates
User Agent	Lat = 41.5225 , Lon = 88.1406
Sensors ✓	☐ Emulate position unavailable

☐ Accelerometer

α: 0

β: 0

Y: 0

Reset

When you click through your website's user experience, you ought to find that the web browser correctly substitutes the test values. Virtually move around the globe as you verify that your web apps work as expected in as many places as you can look up and test.

When looking at a model globe representing good ol' planet Earth, we can sometimes see imaginary lines drawn from top to bottom all the way around. These vertical lines are called "longitude." Wrapping around the globe are lines drawn horizontally called "latitude." You can see these lines cross one another, roughly mapping out the world in a convenient array of boxes. When you're looking up lats and lons, notice that there's a difference between measurements in decimal degrees (want) and decimal minutes (do not want). Complex in detail but easy in theory!

If you happen to know the `navigator.geolocation()` function as well as I do or you think like a veteran software engineer and constantly ask, "What will go wrong?" you know there are error conditions that can pop up. Some are random hardware-related issues—like when the phone can't talk to a nearby cell phone tower. In this case, the JavaScript function simply fails one time. A more blocking, unhappy path is when a user denies permission to find out their current position. How rude! Don't they know our app is trying to help them? In any event, there are error conditions our JavaScript needs to handle to ensure the website doesn't fall apart.

Writing that code isn't too difficult, but testing can be a trial unless we take advantage of the Google mobile emulation tools and check the option "Emulator position unavailable."

Let's write a simple webpage with JavaScript, using the function that returns our browser's location.

```
<!DOCTYPE html>

<html>
<head lang="en">
    <title>Geo Location Test</title>
    <meta name="viewport"
        content="width=device-width, initial-scale=1.0">
</head>

<body>

<script type="application/javascript">

    function geoLocSuccess(position) {
        console.log('latitude[' + position.coords.latitude +
            ']...longitude[' + position.coords.longitude + ']');
    }

    function geoLocFailure(error) {
        console.log('Error callback [' + error.message + ']');
    }

    navigator.geolocation.getCurrentPosition(geoLocSuccess, geoLocFailure);

</script>

</body>
```

When you run this in your browser, ensure the developer tools are open, particularly the console. That's important for showing what information comes back successfully or failing because of the printing command `console.log`.

If it's a success, you'll see something like this:

```
latitude[32.96104]. . .longitude[-97.00416779999999]
```

One type of error condition occurs when the user denies location services:

```
Error callback [User denied Geolocation]
```

Another type of error condition occurs when it's not possible for the browser to get the current location for some reason:

```
Error callback [PositionUnavailable]
```

When you run your website and the browser is simulating a geolocation failure, you can casually test your code to ensure that it does the correct detection and reporting to your user. Sometimes it's an accident, and they'll be happy to have the heads-up along with direction on how to fix the problem. Either way, you'll be happy to know your code behaves as you expect it to. Powerful developer tools that come with modern browsers will make your work easier and your development life happier.

Developer Tools for Mobile or Desktop

DEVELOPER TOOLS—ELEMENTS

Opening the developer tools first reveals the "Elements" tab. If you've never used this, pause a minute and give yourself some time to look around. It's a lot to take in, and it looks highly technical at first, but it's not. Use it to inspect your own website to get a feel for the tool. You'll quickly recognize the underlying structure of your document laid out in HTML.

Notice that the HTML shown in the tool does not look literally like the code you wrote. Instead, this is the current representation of the DOM tree in HTML form. This represents how your browser sees your document.

Pass your mouse across the HTML layout and see the corresponding elements on your document page highlight. This quickly provides hints about what code represents what page rendering. Double-click on various parts of the HTML to edit an element in line. You can change things as you look at them. This is a fantastic way of visually inspecting your website and tweaking it to see if changes are better or worse.

Double-clicking on attributes lets you make changes like these:

- Element IDs

- Class names

- Default text values

There are editing modes in the developer tools in which you can edit an entire block of HTML wholesale, adding and removing as much detail as you desire. Change the entire section of code if you want to experiment. Pull blocks of HTML up and down the page by dragging and dropping them. This tool is powerful and worth playing around in to get a feel for how much can be done. Discover more on your own over time.

You'll often turn to this tool just as a mechanic looks under the hood of a running car to get a feel for what's moving regularly and what's misfiring. It's an incredibly useful introductory tool, and it's something I encourage you to pick up and make your own.

DEVELOPER TOOLS—STYLES

Pairing nicely with the "Elements" panel is the "Styles" panel to its right. For every HTML element on your document, you'll see its CSS rules. We've reviewed previously how important modifying the structural layout of a page is. We must also remember that the style is important because it declares how each element is finally rendered.

Styles come in a few categories of rules, and their order is subtly represented as a stack of boxes:

- The bottom-most boxes are default styles, built into the web browser itself. Given no custom rules, these are the basic ones the browser uses. For example, if you don't define a text color yourself, it defaults to black. Often they're referred to as the "user agent stylesheet."

- The next section of boxes is explicitly declared in your .CSS files as you've crafted your website's look. These are the ones you've written for element type, element by ID, or class names. You'll see them stacked on top of each other as they're layered and mixed as applied to each HTML element. Editing these applies to the basic class and ripples through each application of class or element type.

- Finally, on the very top are styles applied to the particular element. This is a fun box because it's one where you can double-click to add and override styles, tweaking code until the display looks exactly as you want it to.

Editing and viewing styles is a great place to dive head first into developer tools, and I recommend you to take the plunge as soon as you can. Changing element styles on the fly provides amazing real-time feedback. Take the guesswork out of typing CSS in your text editor by designing in the browser. People once considered this an advanced technique, but it's becoming commonplace because it's so easily accomplished. Take time to poke and pull at your site until it's to your liking.

When you're finished changing things, don't forget to record all of your changes in your original source code files back in the text editor. Working in the browser is seductively hands on, but that work is fleeting. Refreshing the page will wipe out all your changes in a fraction of a second.

DEVELOPER TOOLS—SOURCES

When you click on the "Sources" tab, you'll see a panel on the left where you can sort through all of the JavaScript files loaded for your website. Double-click on any of them and the source code is shown in the middle panel. Click on any line number in the left column to set a breakpoint. Breakpoints tell the browser to stop progress if that logic is executed—usually triggered by user interaction. Why use breakpoints? Because when one hits, you can take advantage of the right-hand panel to:

• Poke around each of your variables to make sure each contains what it ought to

- See the list of functions called as a stack from bottom to top, oldest to most recent, ensuring your logic is triggered in order as you expect them

- Manage breakpoints for your JavaScript, DOM changes, and AJAX (asynchronous JavaScript and XML) requests

```
Q  Elements  Network  Sources  Timeline  Profiles  Resources  Audits  Console
Sources  Content scripts  Snippets      AnnaSpellingWords.js?v=1.5 ×
▼ www.annaspellingwords.com        50  }                                          ▼ Watch Expressions        + C
  ▼ resources                      51                                               masterList.length: 16
    ▼ code                         52                                              ▼ Call Stack        □ Async
      Analytics.js                 53   function initListChoices() {                 AnnaSpellingWords.js?v=1.5:64
      AnnaSpellingWords.js?v=1.5   54     var $list = $('#MasterList');              cbListChange
    ▶ css                          55     var numLists = masterList.length;
    (index)                        56     var i, listOption;                         x.event.dispatch  jquery.js:4676
  ▶ ajax.googleapis.com            57                                                y.handle          jquery.js:4360
  ▶ www.google-analytics.com       58     for (i = 0; i < numLists; i++) {
                                    59       listOption = '<option value="' + i + '">' + masterList[i   Paused on a JavaScript breakpoint.
                                    60       $list.append(listOption);
                                    61     }                                        ▼ Scope Variables
                                    62                                              ▼ Local
                                    63     $list.on('change', function cbListChange() {   ▶ this: select#MasterList
                                    64       listIndex = $(this).val();             ▶ Closure
                                    65       initSpellingTest(masterList[listIndex]);  ▶ Global         Window
                                    66       scrollToPageTop();
                                    67     });                                      ▼ Breakpoints
                                    68   }                                          ☑ AnnaSpellingWords.js?v=1.5:64
                                    69                                                $(this).val();
                                    70                                              ☑ AnnaSpellingWords.js?v=1.5:1...
                                    71   function initSpellingTest(SpellingTest) {    .html('&#215;');
                                    72     var i, prefix, wordIndex, wordEntry;     ▶ DOM Breakpoints
                                    73     var numWords = SpellingTest.words.length;  ▶ XHR Breakpoints        +
                                    74     var randomWords = JSON.parse(JSON.stringify(SpellingTest.w  ▶ Event Listener Breakpoints
                                    75                                              ▶ Workers
                                    76     $('#SpellList').empty();
                                    77
                                    78     for (i = 0; i < numWords; i++) {
                                    79
                                    {}  Line 64, Column 1

Console  Search  Emulation  Rendering
⊘  ▽  <top frame>              ▼
> masterList[0]
< ▼ Object {title: "Friday May 2, 2014", lesson: "Contractions", words: Array[10]}
      lesson: "Contractions"
      title: "Friday May 2, 2014"
    ▶ words: Array[10]
    ▶ __proto__: Object
> arguments.length
< 1
>
```

Source code inspection is only useful if you've written some of it or know the libraries that you have included. Some of the open-source libraries that you pull into your website—such as jQuery, perhaps—may have been optimized (minified) for final production work. That means all of the spaces and whitespace that humans need for properly reading it are gone because the computer and browser don't require them, and deleting that extra information reduces the overall file size. These are hard to read, and debugging them isn't particularly useful. When you do want to see what's going on inside your favorite open-source library, look for versions of it that aren't minified or compressed or that otherwise tell you they're useful for development and debugging.

When you do write JavaScript, look to this section of the developer tools to help you gain understanding on how it's called by your website. Use breakpoints to stop your code in its tracks so you can look around and see what has happened and what hasn't happened. There are buttons that let you step through it a single line at a time to see how every instruction changes the world. Some let you step into a function to see all of its internal workings, but if you know for a fact it's behaving well, step over it.

Some of these words will sound technical and peculiar because they're from the domain of software engineers. It's true, but the more you fearlessly approach them, the more clearly you'll understand them over time. It's worth it and will empower you to be a better teammate and maker. This is definitely an intermediate-level tool, so don't put pressure on yourself to understand it all at once.

DEVELOPER TOOLS—NETWORK

Monitoring which files come across the network from your website to your browser is an advanced technique. Have a look at it for sure, but don't hassle yourself if looking at this page isn't immediately obvious or interesting to you. In many ways, it's a finishing-touch tool. As an artist and designer, you build out your site; when you find that it feels sluggish, you and your engineer can take some time to look in here to find which files are slow to serve.

Q | Elements | Network | Sources Timeline Profiles Resources Audits Console

● ⊘ ▽ ⊞ ☐ Preserve log ☑ Disable cache

Name	Met..	St..	Type	Initiator	Size	Time	Timeline
jquery.js	GET	200	text/javascript	Other	70.5 KB	160 ms	
jquery.min.map	GET	200	application/json	www.annaspellingwords.com..	49.8 KB	143 ms	
complete.m4a	GET	206	application/octet-stream	www.annaspellingwords.com..	35.6 KB	493 ms	
wrong.m4a	GET	206	application/octet-stream	www.annaspellingwords.com..	31.8 KB	395 ms	
correct.m4a	GET	206	application/octet-stream	www.annaspellingwords.com..	29.7 KB	411 ms	
jquery.min.js	GET	200	text/javascript	www.annaspellingwords.com..	29.1 KB	91 ms	
whats.m4a	GET	206	application/octet-stream	Other	23.6 KB	262 ms	
shes.m4a	GET	206	application/octet-stream	Other	22.5 KB	295 ms	
hes.m4a	GET	206	application/octet-stream	Other	18.1 KB	242 ms	
heres.m4a	GET	206	application/octet-stream	Other	17.4 KB	274 ms	
im.m4a	GET	206	application/octet-stream	Other	17.1 KB	340 ms	
thats.m4a	GET	206	application/octet-stream	Other	16.8 KB	342 ms	
dont.m4a	GET	206	application/octet-stream	Other	16.6 KB	255 ms	
master.json	GET	200	application/json	jquery.js:7845	16.4 KB	406 ms	
ga.js	GET	200	text/javascript	Analytics.js:11	15.8 KB	98 ms	
theres.m4a	GET	206	application/octet-stream	Other	15.1 KB	137 ms	
isnt.m4a	GET	206	application/octet-stream	Other	14.6 KB	335 ms	
doesnt.m4a	GET	206	application/octet-stream	Other	13.3 KB	318 ms	
AnnaSpellingWords.js?v=1.5	GET	200	application/x-javascript	www.annaspellingwords.com..	6.1 KB	224 ms	
AnnaSpellingWords.css?v=1.2	GET	200	text/css	www.annaspellingwords.com..	3.5 KB	223 ms	
www.annaspellingwords.com	GET	200	text/html	Other	1.9 KB	137 ms	
Analytics.js	GET	200	application/x-javascript	www.annaspellingwords.com..	758 B	232 ms	
__utm.gif?utmwv=5.5.3&utms=1&utmn..	GET	200	image/gif	ga.js:63	404 B	84 ms	

23 requests | 466 KB transferred

What happens when the browser records files brought across? What's it mean? You'll see a list of them, and you can take notice of the size for sure, but in a way, size doesn't matter. It's all about speed and how long it takes to drag them across. Any file that takes more than 500 ms, which is half a second, is something to notice. Small delays add up over time, and before you know it, you have a slow site on your hands.

When a website takes too much time to respond to user input, you can expect those users to leave. My sales friend Kristine reminds me that "time kills deals." You don't want a slow site to make your customers drift away to the competition.

Clicking on the "Time" column, you can sort the list of resources by speed in descending or ascending order. Use the one that makes the most sense to you.

Name	Met...	St...	Type	Initiator	Size	Time	▼ Timeline
complete.m4a	GET	206	application/octet-stream	www.annaspellingwords.com ...	35.6 KB	493 ms	
correct.m4a	GET	206	application/octet-stream	www.annaspellingwords.com ...	29.7 KB	411 ms	
master.json	GET	200	application/json	jquery.js:7845	16.4 KB	406 ms	
wrong.m4a	GET	206	application/octet-stream	www.annaspellingwords.com ...	31.8 KB	395 ms	
thats.m4a	GET	206	application/octet-stream	Other	16.8 KB	342 ms	
im.m4a	GET	206	application/octet-stream	Other	17.1 KB	340 ms	
isnt.m4a	GET	206	application/octet-stream	Other	14.6 KB	335 ms	
doesnt.m4a	GET	206	application/octet-stream	Other	13.3 KB	318 ms	
shes.m4a	GET	206	application/octet-stream	Other	22.5 KB	295 ms	
heres.m4a	GET	206	application/octet-stream	Other	17.4 KB	274 ms	
whats.m4a	GET	206	application/octet-stream	Other	23.6 KB	262 ms	
dont.m4a	GET	206	application/octet-stream	Other	16.6 KB	255 ms	
hes.m4a	GET	206	application/octet-stream	Other	18.1 KB	242 ms	
Analytics.js	GET	200	application/x-javascript	www.annaspellingwords.com ...	758 B	232 ms	
AnnaSpellingWords.js?v=1.5	GET	200	application/x-javascript	www.annaspellingwords.com ...	6.1 KB	224 ms	
AnnaSpellingWords.css?v=1.2	GET	200	text/css	www.annaspellingwords.com ...	3.5 KB	223 ms	
jquery.js	GET	200	text/javascript	Other	70.5 KB	160 ms	⬤
jquery.min.map	GET	200	application/json	www.annaspellingwords.com ...	49.8 KB	143 ms	
theres.m4a	GET	206	application/octet-stream	Other	15.1 KB	137 ms	
www.annaspellingwords.com	GET	200	text/html	Other	1.9 KB	137 ms	
ga.js	GET	200	text/javascript	Analytics.js:11	15.8 KB	98 ms	
jquery.min.js	GET	200	text/javascript	www.annaspellingwords.com ...	29.1 KB	91 ms	
__utm.gif?utmwv=5.5.3&utms=1&utmn...	GET	200	image/gif	ga.js:63	404 B	84 ms	

23 requests | 466 KB transferred

What if you find files that you suspect are taking too long? What are some of the things you can do to make them more efficient?

- If it's a .PNG image file, you can convert it to a .JPG for better compression if it's completely opaque. If transparency is important, tools such as PNG Crush exist that will squeeze every last extraneous bit away.

- If it's a JavaScript library, you can look for tools that minify it to squeeze it down, removing the whitespace and simplifying variable names that humans need but computers do not.

- If it's other heavy resources such as audio and video, you might find ways to delay loading them until the user calls for their playback.

Q/A experts will enjoy getting to know this tool.

Measure your website's transmission speeds over time. Performance monitoring is a key discipline in today's world because quick response is coveted. Users waiting more than a few seconds will become impatient, and in a few seconds more, they may become lost as they move on to the next website.

I've found that optimizing doesn't matter until I can reliably measure what I'm going to change. I need to know before, after, and the difference between to understand if my tweaks and tunes are a help or a hindrance. Make measurement as easy as possible, because easier means it's done more often.

FINDING INSPIRATION AND ANSWERS FROM OTHERS

"This website is amazing. The animations and interaction are fantastic. How did they do that?" You probably ask yourself this question daily. I know I do.

Fortunately, Google Chrome lets you right-click on any page element to perform an "Inspect Element," which opens Developer Tools straight to its details. Of course, you'll find nearby the CSS "Styles" panel. Flooding your brain are all the things that make a cool-looking site tick. Finally, looking around in the "Sources" tab, you'll see any JavaScript code supporting dynamic interactions. Use these tools to understand what other highly skilled professionals have done before you.

Hopefully creators won't think this is underhanded, theft, or unsporting to a level of cheating. From my perspective, there's a long tradition of copying masters to obtain one's own education. As a student, I grew up hearing stories of amateur artists visiting museums to witness the great treasure troves of art hanging upon the walls. Displays of great work are the examples students take for understanding color, shape, and composition. Taking basic supplies to copy the paintings is a well-known convention. Practice makes perfect, and we might as well have perfection as our target.

I've done this many times in recent years as a diversion and escape to practice my hand skills. With a drawing book and pencil in my back pocket, I've roamed the many halls of my local Dallas Museum of Art, stopping long enough to quickly sketch whatever inspires me. I've done the same when it comes to websites. Of course, our clear warning in this regard for our professional lives comes from Pablo Picasso, who said:

Good artists copy; great artists steal.

Surely we can say that mimicry of a single site's style is weak, but surveying many to get a sense of style and overarching themes and techniques is a better use of our time and effort. Use your browser's inspection tool to find out what the trends of your day are. Tease out specific techniques from many websites to improve your skills. Observe everyone to see what's most important for you at that moment.

CHROME CANARY

In my opinion, one of the best-kept secrets in the web development community is Google Chrome Canary. Of course it's not literally a secret, but it's not a particularly common program that we hear of people installing. I can only say it's obscure. That's on purpose, I believe, because using it takes the right stuff in a designer, developer, and engineer. Canary is built nightly from the latest code its programmers submit. Feature changes happen nearly every day without stop, and you might be surprised what you find.

Someone could say that's troublesome. It introduces randomness and variables that make building software difficult. Fair enough, but when I think of it more, it's amazing. I get to see in beta form what's going to happen several months before final release to the public. I can preview their changes to ensure my website holds up to future expectations.

Even better, the Canary browser takes on changes in the development tools. At the writing of this book, my Canary-based developer tools look a far sight different than what people see in widely used Chrome. Does Canary's occasional updates to itself bring some glitches? Sure, but problems rarely remain for long, and the valuable benefit of seeing what's to come is well worth the time taken to incorporate it as a powerful entry in our toolbox.

Its programmers have spent time making Canary separate from Chrome. Both browsers can be installed and open at the same time without conflict. In the unlikely event you ever see Canary do something that's unexpected, you can simply run Chrome. Comparing the results might reveal if the bug is in fact a feature change according to design. I often keep my Chrome browser installed as my routine personal browser because it's totally stable and reliable.

Now that you know about this, will you look for it to better test your work and receive developer tools before your competition does? You might wonder if other major browsers do the same service for the community. In fact, you can easily search to find that Mozilla does the same for Firefox, Opera offers fresh builds, WebKit serves as the foundation for Safari, and so too does Internet Explorer. Check for these in your favorite search engine using keywords such as "developer preview" and "nightly build."

Alternatives

There are many feature-rich options for tooling in this arena. In fact, it's almost to the point that it's a matter of taste. If one of the major web browsers suits your needs for whatever reason, you're going to have great success using it. If there's some particular aspect of Internet Explorer, Firefox, Safari, or Chrome that makes your creative workflow explode, then by all means use it. Most have the basic abilities that will make you more productive in seeing, finding, and fixing bugs on webpages or web apps.

Whatever tool you choose, please take time to learn it thoroughly. Use it every day and take a chance to figure out one more thing it does. This is one of the tools that can separate you from the inexperienced masses in the industry, distance you from the competition, and help raise the game of you and your team.

Browse Sites and Debug Your Own

Browsing the web is surely a fascinating pursuit. There's so much content contained within its boundless frontier that it's inconceivable to wrap my brain around it. All of the human emotional reactions are stuffed inside it to a point of overflowing. Mixed alongside those are intellectual reports and data sets of factual evidence, all within reach. In the very same tool that we use to browse through these pages, flowing along links loosely coupling sites to more sites, we have the ability to stop and see how they're constructed.

Looking at other people's work gives us insight into their techniques and craft. Library choices, conventions, and technical trade-offs are learning lessons for us. Reflecting on what others in our industry are doing surely informs our thinking to reinforce good choices and reconsider flawed ones.

Inspecting our own sites leads to better work that's more functional, reliable, and, whenever possible, simpler. When we decide that work is done, it ought to be bug free and good enough to go out to the customer. We can always find new bugs and fix them with updates, but at the time, we need to have put in enough testing during our creative work cycle to feel confident enough to release.

Interactively examining your HTML layout, CSS rules, and JavaScript logic is the only way to assuredly reach a conclusion that work is done enough to confidently ship out and deploy to the public with your name on it.

All of the modern web browsers are much more than page readers. This chapter brings to light many of the things that Google Chrome can do, because I find it useful enough that I want to explain what it does for me and what problems you can solve with it. When you take the time to investigate any other major modern web browser, you'll see that it has many of the capabilities of Chrome and some that it lacks. We can admit it feels as though there's too much to learn when it comes to front-end web development. Don't let all of the options in the community confuse you with a constant flood of choices. I think it's fine to specialize with a tool until you know it so well that it's a reliable go-to. Whatever browser you choose, realize that it is a powerful tool you ought to invest in learning through constant use.

CHAPTER 9

Surviving CSS by Thriving With Sass

How CSS Is Used for Responsive Design

Three core programming languages drive the client-facing experience for all the websites found on the Internet: HTML, JavaScript, and CSS. You might not realize that every time you fire up an editor and write a few lines in any of those, you're programming. It's true. Modern, hands-on designers and artists are programming more than ever, and forward-thinking programmers are considering design and composition. CSS is a core technology of the modern web experience that we literally can't live without. Sometimes I think I can't possibly live another day with it.

CSS is truly incredible because it was created with the intention of serving two audiences—artists and engineers—and apparently it aggravates everyone. Artists and designers using CSS think it looks too much like code. Coders reading CSS think it looks like a twisted pile of spaghetti. CSS is so important that many smart people are interested in thinking about changing it. Projects have sprung up on the Internet and communities have formed up around them, actively using replacement tech and supporting its growth. How can such a thing happen if CSS is crucial? Why replace it?

"Replacing" might be a strong way to put it. Perhaps enabling CSS's improvement, encouraging it to be the best it can be, and accepting its flaws with helpful advice are what the community is doing. In fact, it shows just how easy it is to make website development easier with new tools. When the open-source community pulls together and deliberates on new conventions, it's a win in my mind.

Three of the most noteworthy CSS preprocessors are LESS, Stylus, and Sass. I'm going to talk about Sass.

Sass is a daily-use item in my development toolbox. It improves the CSS language by embracing and extending it with opinions on how to make consistent structural choices across your pages by:

- Creating drop-in modules instead of one-offs

- Declaring colors and sizes once instead of hard-coding them everywhere

- Organizing your work so that it reads clearly as it scales up over time

Why do people think improving CSS is important? Why isn't it good enough for us now? Years ago, HTML and CSS were invented for marking up documents for research scientists sharing their results. At the time, it was revolutionary, but that legacy leaves us with limited ability. Why? It's limiting because we're creative dreamers and relentless builders. Modern websites are mini programs with animations, workflows, dynamic response, and customer choice. It's an interactive experience instead of static presentation. Interactions rarely happen on traditional desktops but instead on unpredictably sized laptops, tablets, and phones.

Building complex modern websites like these demands power tools to get them up and running by creating conventions that are maintained over time. Maintenance is important because websites built with focused planning become valuable investments for companies. Updating them with new content, additional pages, and even wholesale refreshing are important options for companies. Consider that a website can live for years touched by the hands and brains of different workers possessing varied levels of skill. The CSS programming language needs help, and the teams writing it deserve support.

As website makers, we talk about CSS all the time. What does "cascading style sheet" really mean? "Style" seems plain enough and "sheets" aren't that confusing, but what's the deal with "cascading"? When multiple styles are applied to an element, the browser figures out how they flow together and finally applies the correct attributes based on their sequence. It's like orchestrating a mass of people to form an orderly line so that they don't fight as they try to pile onto the same place all at once. General styles are overridden by more specific styles. Multiple styles can apply different values to the same attribute of an element, and the browser must apply them in order.

HOW SASS CAN BE USED FOR RESPONSIVE DEVELOPMENT

Let's jump right in and have a look at some typical Sass code. Observe how it looks like CSS combined with some of the variables and math that you might recognize from a programming language such as JavaScript. Web browsers can't read this file, but instead, the Sass tool reads this and writes out plain old CSS. Software engineers call this type of tool a preprocessor. A tool reads in Sass files and outputs CSS. We might refer to Sass as a metalanguage because it embraces CSS while extending it into far-reaching paths.

```scss
$phoneSize: 568px;
$tabletMinSize: $phoneSize + 1;
$tabletPortrait: 768px;
$laptopSize: 960px;

$screenThumbWidth: 256px;
$screenThumbHeight: 192px;
$screenThumbPhoneScale: 0.75;
$screenThumbLaptopScale: 1.25;

.picture-group {
  .picture-entry {

    @media screen and (max-width: $phoneSize) {
    text-align: center;
    }
  }

  img {
    width: $screenThumbWidth;
    height: $screenThumbHeight;

    @media screen and (max-width: $phoneSize) {
      margin: 0 auto;
      margin-bottom: 10px;
    }

    @media screen and (min-width: $tabletMinSize) and
      (max-width: $tabletPortrait) {
      width: $screenThumbWidth * $screenThumbPhoneScale;
      height: $screenThumbHeight * $screenThumbPhoneScale;
    }

    @media screen and (min-width: $laptopSize) {
      width: $screenThumbWidth * $screenThumbLaptopScale;
      height: $screenThumbHeight * $screenThumbLaptopScale;
    }
  }
}
```

Sass starts building on what you know about CSS, slightly shifting your expectations in a dozen different ways. Putting together their amazing combinations empowers you to craft websites better than ever before. Diving into Sass can start simply for you because it's compatible with CSS. Looking into Sass, you can pull that one thing that makes you curious and solves a distinct problem you encounter daily. Use that thing often, and as your skill increases, your confidence will increase as well. Then reach for the next feature and bring it into your creative workflow as a turbo boost. This chapter is dedicated to introducing artists and designers to some of the most practical parts of Sass.

Creative leaders may want to tag a curious individual on your team to go off and experiment with Sass for a few days or for a few hours a day for a week. Let them explore how many aspects of it will help your team and come back with a brief show-and-tell over lunch. Let it be informal, but purposefully dedicate time to it with all your people present and receptive toward learning from the sharing. See if the lesson helps your team move forward with increased capacity. Use this chapter to guide your forward-thinking adventurer while learning about this intriguing technology.

CSS IS DIFFICULT TO WRITE AND MAINTAIN

CSS is a programming language. Writing it is super simple—you do it all day long. Writing *good* CSS is crazy hard. If you've ever tried to make big sweeping changes across an existing CSS codebase, you know how tricky and unmanageable bad CSS can be. Our goal is to write clean-looking CSS that's easy to read and update. This is a challenge. Not impossible, but surely complicated, because as a programming language, CSS offers no formal opinions on organization—at least not to the extent I expect to see given my career as a software engineer.

Because I've been programming for a little more than 30 years now, more than some of my teammates have been alive, I have expectations from the languages I choose to use for solving interesting problems. Exactly what qualities have I come to expect from a programming language? Here are some of the high-level qualities missing from CSS that I've come to expect:

- **Hierarchy**—things relate to other things, and it's good to declare that with left-aligned whitespace, for example, showing dependent "children" inside owning "parents"
- **Encapsulation**—don't let code logic and data settings escape from a thing by leaking out into the global space occupied by other things that are completely unrelated and don't care
- **Composition**—make up new things by building them up from working parts and reliable pieces pulled from other successfully constructed things

I've found that when programming languages have these ideals built into their syntax and way of thinking, it makes my job easier and raises my chance of success. Can a team of A players do a perfectly fine job crafting a portion of their project using plain CSS even though it lacks those features? I must answer yes because I'm a tireless optimist and have seen the power of creative and skilled people overcome barriers in the face of constraint. I've seen it happen on many occasions in my career, and joining up with teams of these high-quality individuals is my great joy.

What if that team of highly skilled, engaged, and dedicated individuals is tired and stressed out from trying to meet aggressive deadlines? What if that teams in fact has a number of rookie members learning how to build and deliver? In that case, CSS's lack of core features for building software in a professional manner hurts. It's all right, because there's good news: Sass exists to help us overcome CSS's weaknesses.

My Favorite Things About Sass

Let me lead you on a tour around my favorite parts of Sass. You'll find your own over time. Allow me to highlight several things for you to learn about in this chapter. These are some of the crystal-clear moments that I expect will help your education with Sass.

VARIABLES

Engineers use variables to hold a value like a number, color, word, or sentence. Naming things is often difficult, but assigning a number or string of letters to descriptive variables tells the reader what the number or color or string does or why it exists. CSS forces us to type font sizes and colors over and over again in our style definitions. Variables start with the $ character followed by letters or numbers that make up the name.

What if you use a particular color a dozen times and it changes due to a branding update? It's a chore seeking and finding all of the places the old value is used to update it. Tedious work certainly brings with it the potential for creating bugs due to human error in completing the mundane task. Putting colors, sizes, and strings in variables helps isolate the values to a single, well-known place. Updates, maintenance, and routine polish ought to be easier in the future or as initial launch development races along. Here's an example of this concept.

```scss
$normalTextColor: #333;
$featureColor: #004a82;

body {
   color: $normalTextColor;
   font-family: 'Arial', 'Helvetica', sans-serif;
}

h1 {
   color: $featureColor;
}
```

IMPORTING/PARTIALS

Breaking big problems into smaller ones often leads to success more quickly. Think of how you probably have many `.html` and `.js` files in your website. Sass lets you break down a single `.CSS` into many `.SCSS` files. Engineers strive to organize their source code in this way, referring to a concept known as single responsibility principle. That concept suggests one file (module or library) does one thing very well. Sass calls a `.SCSS` file that handles a particular part of your overall style rules a partial. Start a `.SCSS` filename with an underscore, and Sass will treat it only as a file another one depends upon and imports. Sass files that don't start with an underscore could be compiled into their own `.CSS`, and that might be wrong for your needs.

Sass extends the CSS `@import` command, allowing you to bring in any number of files, or partials, into a main `.SCSS` file. Ideally you'll plan these well, allowing you to build them once and use them throughout your company on many websites. The concept of reuse is a powerful one, as your hard work on one project turbo boosts others. Here's an example of how a main file might look:

```scss
@import 'reset';
@import 'typography';
@import 'color_palette';
@import 'grid';
@import 'buttons';
@import 'forms';
@import 'lists';
```

While reading this code snippet, please realize that the Sass tool will look for and find files named like this: `_reset.scss` and `_grid.scss` that match what is written above. When your Sass is processed, consisting of a collection of one or more .SCSS files, it creates a .CSS file containing all the style rules made ready for a web browser to read and render. The Sass tool has an output style parameter that tells it how to format the CSS. Using the compressed style saves as much space as possible, making it nearly impossible for a human to read but making it as efficient as possible for quickly transmitting from your web server to your customer. Efficient file transfer is important because most people have a data plan with their cell services, and conserving their data budget whenever feasible is the best choice. Not to mention quick load time means more satisfied customers.

NESTING/HIERARCHY

Engineers like hierarchy. Entire ideas such as object-oriented programming are based around the concept of hierarchy. In design, composition is how visual relationships are shown. Sass offers nesting as a way of writing code with hierarchy and showing relation. Tucking away styles inside other ones with indenting lets us more easily communicate those tricky relationships to other human beings. Others could be teammates or our future selves who have long forgotten code we wrote.

One of the aspirations is ensuring this code looks as rational as possible. Our goal should be writing source code that provides the entire context and meaning a skilled reader needs to understand what the author intended.

```
#social-list {
    list-style-type: none;

    li {
        float: left;
        padding-right: 20px;
        width: 33%;
    }

    li:last-child {
        padding: 0;
    }
}
```

Here's another example with special notation. Notice the ampersand (&) symbol starting the `:hover` and `:active` rules. The ampersand is simply a reference to the parent selector. Using it keeps the Sass code clean and concise looking.

```
a {
    color: $normalTextColor;
    text-decoration: none;

    &:hover {
        color: $featureColor;
    }

    &:active {
        color: $featureDarkColor;
    }
}
```

MATH

As an author of CSS, you know lots of numbers are floating around your code. Sizes could be in pixels, offsets in percentages, and colors in hex. Numbers are made for math, and Sass helps you perform math in your CSS. Add, subtract, divide, and multiply are available.

Why would you want to do math in the middle of styles? Think about design being about composition and visual relationships between elements. One rule could have a property 25% bigger than another, or starting height with extra pixels added.

```
$mobileSize: 568px;
$tabletMinSize: $mobileSize + 1;

$badgeWidth: 200px;
$badgeWidthPhone: $badgeWidth * 0.50;
$badgeWidthTablet: $badgeWidth * 0.75;
```

Another simple case is bumping over a group of elements by a few pixels. During a polish pass, you could quickly adjust the right or left attributes by typing +6, then +23, and then +38, working elements around the page while refreshing your browser and watching the results. Once satisfied with your fine-tuning, add up the numbers and keep the final ones.

FUNCTIONS

Sass offers a collection of functions for processing numbers. Functions are more complex than the common math operations because they cover a range of needs but ought to be relatable because they're practical. Ultimately, they solve design problems and that makes them concrete and real. For example, use a Sass-provided function called darken to tweak a base color for a bottom-edge shadow:

```
$featureColor: #004a82;
$featureColorDark: darken($featureColor, 15%);
```

Look through the Sass documentation for more on using this function. Review all the others they have. Many more exist for tweaking colors, changing text, processing numbers, and operating on sets of data.

```
http://sass-lang.com/documentation/Sass/Script/Functions.html
```

Again, start with a few things that make sense to you because they solve a problem you have. Use a few until you gain complete confidence. Then reach for a few more and incorporate them into your workflow. Keep the things that work and replace those that don't.

MEDIA QUERIES

Responsive web development demands use of media queries for influencing how HTML tags are rendered by their applied styles. Sass helps organize media queries by tucking them underneath their tags and classes. This makes code look more beautiful because it's organized and rational looking. The left-hand spacing that pushes rules to the right lets you clearly see relationships. Mindful organization from the start of a project always makes jobs go better and sets everyone up for success into future maintenance. You'll notice this is another example of nesting that the Sass tool provides.

Here's an example of a style rule written in Sass that shows two media query rules for a tag with a specific identity. The first shows it at a smaller size for a phone. The second gives it a larger size for tablets. Notice how the code is self-documenting, with the use of variables instead of hard-coded numbers. As opposed to using a pixel number in the media query, it assigns the number to a well-named variable. The clear variable name describes what it is and shows why it's used.

```scss
$mobileSize: 568px + 10;
$tabletMinSize: $mobileSize + 1;
$tabletMaxSize: 960px;

iframe#trailer {
  @media screen and (max-width: $mobileSize) {
    width: 300px;
    height: 169px;
  }

  @media screen and (min-width: $tabletMinSize) and
    (max-width: $tabletMaxSize) {
    width: 560px;
    height: 315px;
  }
}
```

MIXINS

Inventing software tools is fantastic because they're infinitely available. No need to reinvent the wheel, as the cliché goes. CSS offers very little support for building tools, and it seems as though cut and paste is the single way to work faster. Engineers have learned the problems with cut and paste. The worst is when changes are needed. How does a teammate update a block of code when it appears six times? By searching for it and changing each one, and if one is missed, it produces a bug. This tactic is error prone because humans get bored with this type of chore. What if you're not entirely sure how many times a block of code was duplicated and across how many files? That's an error-prone situation as well. What if a copied block was changed a little bit, making it look different enough to make a teammate doubt whether they ought to make a change?

Sass has the perfect way to reuse a snippet of CSS source code. Once you've crafted your code, wrap it up into a mixin. Use it over and over again throughout your .SCSS files. Mixins are referenced wherever you want the associated CSS to expand into place. Some good examples for writing a mixin include:

- Vendor prefixes for an emerging CSS standard such as CSS3 rounded borders or upcoming animation support
- Visual design from a style guide
- Often-used hacks such as a clearfix routine

Defining and using a mixin looks like this:

```scss
$primaryCallColor: #00BAEE;
@mixin heroTitle {
    color: $primaryCallColor;
    font: {
        family: Verdana, Arial, sans-serif;
        size: 64px;
        weight: bold;
    }
    border: 1px solid black;
    padding: 10px;
}

h1 {
    @include heroTitle;
    margin: 20px;
}
```

Although the mixin uses a few hard-coded numbers rather than well-named variables for the padding and font size, the fact that they're contained within the mixin helps hide them away from spilling out into the file. Anytime that mixin is changed, simply running the Sass tool on your .SCSS files guarantees updates are distributed throughout your project wherever the mixin is included. No need to guess where they are. That might not seem important as a project begins because it's fresh in your mind and you can flip to references quickly. As time goes on, however, a team's collective memory becomes fuzzy, and letting Sass help is an advantage. No need to search and replace throughout a collection of code files, since a quick run of the tool rebuilds your .CSS file.

COMPRESSION

As an engineer, I talk and debate about compression at least once a week. I believe everything can be made smaller. Smaller is nearly always better when it comes to modern electronics and nearly always better when applied to resources sent from your web server to your customer's device. Images can be compressed, JavaScript can be compressed, and so too can .CSS files. Sass has you covered in this category because the .SCSS files can be written out to a final combined file written as small as possible. It does that by throwing away as much white space as possible. Humans benefit from spaces and line breaks when reading, but web browsers simply don't care and read it without hesitation.

Sass writes out your combined .CSS file in what it calls the output style. Without telling it anything special, it writes a file with whitespace and line breaks making it human readable, and the largest possible. For example, given this typical media query snippet, which is easily read by any human teammate and is uncompressed, weighing in at 320 bytes in size:

```scss
$mobileSize: 568px + 10;
$tabletMinSize: $mobileSize + 1;
$tabletMaxSize: 960px;

iframe#trailer {
  @media screen and (max-width: $mobileSize) {
    width: 300px;
    height: 169px;
  }

  @media screen and (min-width: $tabletMinSize) and
    (max-width: $tabletMaxSize) {
    width: 560px;
    height: 315px;
  }
}
```

Compiling it to a default .CSS file, you'll see written out code that's 226 bytes long and looks like this:

```css
@media screen and (max-width: 578px) {
  iframe#trailer {
    width: 300px;
    height: 169px; } }

@media screen and (min-width: 579px) and (max-width: 973px) {
  iframe#trailer {
    width: 560px;
    height: 315px; } }
```

The same code written out with compressed style produces a .CSS file only 185 bytes long that looks like this:

```
@media screen and (max-width:
578px){iframe#trailer{width:300px;height:169px}}@media
screen and (min-width: 579px) and (max-width:
973px){iframe#trailer{width:560px;height:315px}}
```

The difference in file compression is almost a 20% saving, and believe me, it adds up over time. Your project's SCSS source code and final CSS are going to be much larger than this elementary example. The more readers that visit your site, the more bandwidth cost you save on sending files to them. It's a win all around, and Sass builds this in from the start.

MODERN COMMENTS

I believe that commenting code can be a weakness. Many people say it is a strength because an author is conveying meaning to future readers. But comments are just another way human beings create bugs. An author tells why they're doing something because the code tells what is being done. Later maintainers end up inserting code, shifting lines up and down, and retrofitting new features. If they didn't maintain the comments as well, then they're all out of date and obsolete. Worse, they're outright incorrect or possibly even near the wrong lines of code.

The next time you write code and feel the need to add comments to explain what is going on, take a moment and consider if the code can be rewritten in a way that doesn't require a comment. Usually the second pass will be better designed.

Modern code writers understand it's best to write code that's self-documenting. That said, Sass offers modern comments that look like // rather than /* */. The double-slash syntax for comments is easier to type, less error prone, and looks far less noisy when reading through source code. Here's an example of modern comments.

```
// baseline preview image size
$screenThumbWidth: 256px;
$screenThumbHeight: 192px;

$screenThumbPhoneScale: 0.75; // 75% for smaller screens
$screenThumbLaptopScale: 1.25; // 125% for larger screens
```

Introductory Way of Using Sass

Assuming you have Sass installed on your work computer (more on that in an upcoming section), you'll have the tool available on the command line. In both OS X and Windows, the tool is called the same and has matching parameters. Here's the basic way of using it:

That produces a final .CSS that combines all the individual .SCSS files given a human-readable file with whitespace and line breaks. It's fine for learning, debugging, and previewing on your work computer as you build up your website and web apps.

Intermediate Way of Using Sass

Compressing your final .CSS file by telling Sass to write it with an efficient output style is next. Building upon how we compiled our style sheet in the previous example, see this next example, which uses a command-line parameter:

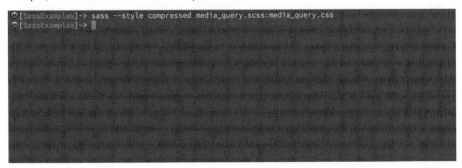

That produces a final .CSS that combines all the individual .SCSS files given a machine-readable file with all unnecessary whitespace and line breaks removed. It's the most space-efficient version that you can have ready for final deployment to your customer-facing web server.

LET SASS HELP

Sass is a tool built to help you. By layering up a level of syntactic sweetness, it improves the restrictive yet verbose CSS we all started learning years ago. You might discover using the

Sass tool is confusing every once in a while. Command-line tools generally receive a negative opinion because they seem to hide their functionality. There are no menus or buttons that obviously reveal their abilities, as a GUI app has. Convention among engineers is making their command-line tools accept the parameter `--help` to offer up reminders. When you issue the command `sass --help`, you'll see a block of text reminding you what the Sass tool can do given parameters. Take advantage of this help while learning the tool to start and periodically as you reach for one of its extended capabilities.

Advanced Way of Using Sass

Making changes in your editor and then swapping over to the command-line window running the Sass tool is fine to start, but it becomes time consuming. It's also error prone because getting in the zone will eventually mean editing and then swapping over to the web browser and wondering why the changes aren't showing when you tap the refresh key. A computer is the best at mindlessly following your orders exactly as you tell it to. Let's tell Sass to watch your SCSS files, and when it sees any of them have changed, it will write a fresh copy of the .CSS. It's easy to use its watch parameter, as seen here:

```
[SassExamples]-> sass media_query.scss:media_query.css
[SassExamples]-> sass --style compresswatch --ed media_query.scss:media_query.css
>>> Sass is watching for changes. Press Ctrl-C to stop.
[Listen warning]:
   Listen will be polling for changes. Learn more at https://github.com/guard/listen#polling-fallback.
>>> Change detected to: media_query.scss
      write media_query.css
```

Automatic tools are great time savers that reduces tedium and the human error that necessarily comes from boredom. Write your Sass code and let the tool figure out when to make a new style sheet.

Sass is a command-line tool. Why do programmers prefer text-based utilities? They seem intimidating and aren't at all user friendly. True, but designing a graphical front end takes time, and the first pass on a tool is always about building a working feature. Many times, command-line tools are easier to snap into build tools like make, grunt, gulp, and Jenkins that add automatic conversions for convenience. Often tools become popular and gain GUIs from other teams that want to make them more accessible for a wider audience.

Organization—Think in Libraries

Thinking in libraries is always a surefire way of helping your teammates, the community, and future you. It's true that working in a real-world local library is a quiet sanctuary that enables concentration and brainpower, but in this case, I don't literally mean think in a library. Libraries are a way programmers package code into useful bundles that others use. Think of a bundle of code as something that you can reach for to benefit from immediately. Instead of making something one off, build it to be used as a drop-in. Software libraries never run out and are always ready to build up a stable foundation that raises up your project or to tap into a tight-fitting space and fill in a missing piece.

Patterns and recipes are other metaphors for quickly describing practical tools that help you build software, but I don't like either of them in this case. A pattern is a cutout that a person must trace around to replicate a shape on a piece of material then cut out for fabrication. Closer is the idea of a recipe, which is an ordered list of directions that tells a person how to pull together ingredients that are combined for a final dish. Neither describes the power of casually bringing in a library that snaps into place and immediately gives you a complete item ready for operation.

If libraries are best known to engineers as bundles of working code, in JavaScript, C, Ruby, Python, whatever, how does that apply to Sass and CSS? The same idea is directly applicable, because CSS is code after all. Once you've built a complete set of styles or even a handful of them, start thinking about how you can save yourself from ever building the same thing again. Invest your time in building new stuff! Don't spend your future tracing over your old lines. Create libraries of solutions to your problems now and forever.

There's the evocative idea of the "lazy programmer" that inspires us to think of how spending a little time researching prior art before jumping into coding can save us from pouring unneeded time into working a problem. Avoiding work sounds like a horrible quality in a teammate, but in the spirit of reuse, I've found it to be one of the finest attributes of smart colleagues.

Who do we create libraries for?

- For our future selves who are overworked and annoyed they can't remember that one time they already solved the same problem
- For our teammates who will proudly call us their favorite creative partners as we help them push forward past an all-too-short deadline
- For our company that can move forward with purpose as all its employees share with one another for greater speed
- For the open-source community to pay back or pay forward, keeping the virtuous circle spinning

Ideally, libraries are started by a single mind with a certain purpose and released to a group, with some working examples testing its features. Written documentation is a definite plus.

From there, others are invited to use it and participate in its future. Libraries make an abstract idea real, and real things can be enhanced. Goals for enhancing a library include:

- Bug fixes for broken aspects
- Optimizations that make slower things faster
- Additional documentation and tests
- Feature enhancements
- Teams learn it and stay smart

Learning a library is a way teams can acquire skill and propel their abilities forward. It's a tool, and like any tool, a Sass library will increase your power and ability.

Creative leaders, encourage your teams to build and maintain libraries. They contain hard-fought solutions to old problems that make future projects easier. Work becomes easier by relieving the stress of remembering past solutions under time constrains. Look to libraries as assets worth investing in. This benefits your entire company over time. They're ways for you to increase delivery capacity as your skilled individual contributors make teams work with intelligence.

Given any particular problem, I could sit down and blast out the code—whatever comes to mind first—and get the job done. As soon as I get something working, I could move on to the next task. Source code written in this way is quickly forgotten because it's impossible to reuse. If I took a little time to write reusable code, I'd be delivering value to my client, reducing the amount of new code my teammates must write, and even helping out future me.

Steve McConnell write, in his thoughtful book, *Code Complete*:

> *"What if I'm just writing code for myself? Why should I make it readable?" Because a week or two from now you're going to be working on another program and think, "Hey! I already wrote this routine last week. I'll just drop in my old tested, debugged, code and save some time." If the code isn't readable, good luck!*
>
> Steve McConnell, *Code Complete: A Practical Handbook of Software Construction* (Redmond: Microsoft Press, 1993, p. 779)

When writing new code, we should seek out readability over everything else. Code is best when it's functional, reliable, sensibly organized, self-commenting, and easily understood by any professional reading it.

INSTALLING SASS

You'll want to install Sass once you've read through this chapter and decided that it's a powerful tool to add to your professional toolbox. Look to the official website for how to install it:

```
http://sass-lang.com/install
```

The Sass site describes two ways of installing Sass: (1) using a GUI app and (2) using the command-line tools. The GUI apps are actually calling the Sass command-line tool behind the scenes. Some are free and others are paid, and all come from third parties building atop Sass. Please pursue one of them if that feels more comfortable to you.

The command-line tool is what is officially supported by the community that builds and improves Sass. Because they are building the command-line edition it will have the most up-to-date improvements first, and apps will try following up behind them. I recommend you install and use the command-line version. Many people think the command line is intimidating because it doesn't casually reveal its capabilities. Look to the Sass documentation on their website, because it reveals all. This chapter has a section showing how to use Sass well enough to propel you through your work.

When you look at their installation website, you'll see a list of apps you can choose. Some run on one or more of the major operating systems. The command-line edition asks for you to first install the programming language Ruby. If you're using a Mac, congrats, you already have Ruby because it comes preinstalled in OS X.

If you've not heard of it, Ruby is a scripting language that powers many successful web servers. The startup community has found that a small team can provide extensive functionality quickly when Ruby is paired up with a library called Rails. Sass makers choose Ruby as the language they want to use for building their tool. Rails isn't involved, but other open-source libraries are. Because they choose Ruby, and that language is on many computers, Sass can be run on them and widely adapted.

Please follow the Sass website instructions for installing their tool. I believe they're clearly written and current. There's no need for this book to duplicate their fine effort.

PROGRAMMERS HAVE (CODE) STYLE

Why does code style matter? Do you need to settle on a convention? Probably not if it's just you writing Sass by yourself. As soon as you mix in other folks, it has a way of becoming more difficult than we want it to. Modern web development is already complicated enough that figuring out the ways of making it simpler ought to be a goal. A key way engineers have found is agreeing on conventions in code style.

If everyone on the team is writing code that looks the same, at least you have that going for you when everything else is getting tough. When all the Sass code looks the same, at least that feels welcoming and consistent when you drop into a file someone else wrote and intend to edit it. Any project of a significant size on any project running a significant time will have a lot of code. Odds are lots of it won't have been originally crafted by your hand, but you will eventually touch it.

What goes into a code convention? Mindfully making choices like these:

- Indents as spaces or tabs

- How to name variables camelCase or snake_case or divided-by-dashes

- The order of attributes in a style definition

- Hierarchy of files and how you break down into files (includes)

- Any external libraries that you want to pull into your project

- How much you abbreviate variable names

Use code reviews to enforce and remind one another about convention details. Use this as a way to initiate new teammates. Teach them by having them look at the best code you've written and fix the worst of it. By the way, all the code ought to be good enough that you're proud to show off it.

Code conventions are similar to design guides. Typical of most art departments, guides keep teams on track, build capacity, and retain consistency among employees. You'll find this even more valuable if you ever need to work with external contractors to help build some of your site. They might have their own style or a complete lack of style, and you'll want them to conform to yours. Some of it is for looks, but it's defensive, too. Have high expectations in quality early and throughout your project.

Craft your own code style guide. Encourage everyone to add to it and improve it over time. Keep it alive, and change it in response to what you've learned. Start with a community-published guide if you don't want to write one. Search on you favorite search site, and you'll find several from which to choose. Pull in the one that strikes you and work from it for a while. Learn what you like and dislike about it and improve it as you work.

Whatever you do, please make a decision as early as possible. You have a choice, and it matters. CSS is one of those things that gets out of control quickly. Sass absorbs some of those troubles, but it can't protect you from everything. In an organization big enough to have multiple teams, they might all want to have a choice in picking their convention, but caution against that. Creative leaders might want consistency across teams and their assigned projects, just as a team would among its members. This might make it easier for employees to cross boundaries and slide between teams. Then they can help when deadlines get crunchy and have an option when they crave a new creative outlet and desire to transfer inside the company.

Sass makes you choose from one of its styles. Look at their website, and you'll see code examples are shown using two distinct syntaxes. One is SCSS, and it is the style I've chosen to write examples in. It borrows heavily from the basic CSS syntax and looks familiar to anyone writing CSS code. Because of the familiar feel, I suggest that you adopt it.

The second syntax choice is called Sass. It offers minimalism by removing most punctuation for clean-looking code. Indentation beginning each line is important because it describes hierarchy and context. It's a more radical interpretation of CSS, and if your team selects it, there will be a learning curve.

DEBUGGING SASS IN CHROME DEVELOPER TOOLS

Finding glitches and fixing them is a recurring theme in this book. A key ability of debugging your code is seeing your source code executing in a browser. When you get to a problem, you can page through your code and see the state of affairs of your program. Browsers know about HTML, JavaScript, and CSS. CSS is naturally the final output of your Sass, but seeing what the CSS looks like in your browser as you step through code isn't the best possible way to diagnose logic errors. When you get to a point where you're writing Sass daily, you'll want to debug within the context of it.

Google's Chrome browser has a working solution for this. It connects the dots between the written CSS output and the original Sass you wrote. A technology called "source map" is what you'll see written when you investigate this topic.

Because this is an advanced lesson, we won't review details about it in this book. It's more than I want to get into now, but please research this tool when you're ready to learn about it. Check out this page for more:

```
https://developer.chrome.com/devtools/docs/css-preprocessors
```

COMMUNITY TOOLS

Libraries are bundles of code that are easily used in present and future projects by you and your team. Lots can be made of them, but in the end, they represent solutions for problems you've already faced and ought to never have to repeat. Whenever possible, think of building up libraries, because the time invested in crafting them now will make working in the future quicker.

The open-source community has assembled many libraries that you can reach for. Like any tool, they amplify your abilities and empower you to better perform your job. I see the additional tools supplementing Sass in two distinct ways:

1. Applications providing graphical user interfaces

2. Frameworks of styles and functions

The Sass install page lists a number of applications that you might prefer over the command-line interface. Here are examples of some of the libraries that provide solutions to responsive design, grid layouts, browser-specific vendor prefixes, animations, and other helpers: Compass, Foundation, Bourbon, Neat, Susy, and Bootstrap.

By now you've looked for solutions to your project glitches and problems using your web search engine of choice. It's good to remember this is an alternative when you and your teammates are stuck trying to solve a problem. There's a good chance someone else has had a similar glitch, fixed it, and documented the solution. Even better, these folks might have productized the fix by publishing a library and posting it on GitHub. Take advantage of prior art if you can, and participate in it by publishing some yourself.

Alternatives to Sass—A Quick Survey

Sass is the subject of this chapter. I've built a case for why you'll want to use it to improve your CSS workflow. I propose that using plain CSS is not enabling and bluntly prevents you from becoming the awesome master of the web universe that you could become. What if you're in the tricky situation where you know you don't want to build a significant website using raw CSS but are unwilling to choose Sass? Are you wondering if there are similar competitive tools that enable you to build better style in your project? Yes, there are a few. Even if you do want to use Sass, you might want to examine these other systems as a competitive review. Determine if there's an advantage to them and how you can apply their lessons to your own work.

Less is a major competitor to Sass. It's also used as a command-line tool, and it's written in JavaScript. Instead of requiring Ruby as Sass does, Less asks you to first install NodeJS so it can run. NodeJS is on all of the major operating systems, and therefore Less is widespread and available to you. Many of the features Sass is well known for appear in Less. Bootstrap is a famous tool, and it uses Less for features such as themes and responsive layout math. The undeniable popularity of Bootstrap may have had a hand in making Less famous in your world. You may also be curious to know that Bootstrap has recently been adapted to use Sass because of its popularity.

NodeJS is mentioned a few times here, and you might have read about it before. It's a version of JavaScript that runs on the server. It powers websites just as PHP, Java, Ruby, and Python do. NodeJS also allows JavaScript to run on a command-line, letting it become a language for tools. It's worth learning about because front-end makers can dabble in back-end work and invent time-saving automation tools.

Stylus is another competitor to Sass that's also built in JavaScript and requires the command-line version of it, NodeJS. This CSS compiler is often paired up with websites built in the NodeJS language. Know that it can be used on its own to generate CSS. Stylus has many of the conveniences found in Sass but diverged in a way by making the language look different. As I read through Stylus code, I think its creators are trying to remove the special characters that make CSS look like a computer language. I believe that their objective in simplifying the language is to inspire more people to take a committed look at it and select it for daily use. Without parentheses, curly braces, colons, and semicolons, some people will say it reads more clearly.

Whatever you do, please consider choosing a tool that offers a time-saving advantage over writing raw CSS. It simply wasn't created with today's complicated websites and web apps in mind. You need assistance in first crafting styles and then maintaining them, and one of these tools will improve your workflow.

Surviving CSS by Thriving With Sass

Given all that's written in this chapter, one might think I dislike CSS to the core of my being. I understand that suspicion, but it's not entirely true. I respect what CSS is capable of, understand what it does well, and admit that it's a core technology of the web browsing experience. I simply want a better tool for you, and as an engineer, I know we can definitely do better. In this case, better means embracing CSS but extending it in a rich direction that its authors couldn't have guessed we'd need in our modern websites. Initially invented for formatting technical papers, CSS is constantly pushed beyond its capability, as websites have evolved from single pages to complex programs.

Dealing with complexity is a constant in software development. I assert that over my career, I've seen that previous problems have indeed become easier, but then we somehow make the job more complex by adding higher expectations. We're adding deeper interactions, richer visual interfaces, and broader support of viewing hardware. Over time, engineers have created ways of thinking about approaches to reduce complication from additional wants. Formal thinking produces mental tools such as:

- **Hierarchy** for better organization and code that is more easily understood

- **Encapsulation** to self-contain work into single responsibilities and solutions

- **Composition** that produces variables, mixins, and libraries for reuse

Don't assume these techniques are the exclusive domain of engineers. Anyone interested should reach for any one or more of these tools and pull them into their creative workflow. Each is empowering and helps solve a classic programming challenge. They can empower you, too. Given what you've learned about Sass, think of how it embodies these approaches and whether they are of concrete benefit to you. Especially reflect on what you've already experienced with years of writing in the CSS language. If plain CSS is good enough for you and your team, then please stay with it.

Now, if you're imagining you need a better alternative, it's time to mindfully consider a change. Evaluating a tool like Sass will become a material competitive advantage for you either as an individual, as a team, or as a company. Whatever you do, intentionally consider building your CSS with a higher-level language that sits on top and compiles down to it. Excellent alternatives to Sass are listed in this chapter, and you'll do well choosing any of them. By picking one of them and incorporating it into your development tool chain, you will become more productive, your team can better share its solutions with itself and others, and you may discover more time to polish your web projects.

CHAPTER 10

Google Analytics

Measuring Your UX With Analytics

Why Are Analytics Important?

So much about making things in the business world is that we need to solve problems for people by providing them value. In turn, we need to make some money—we need to profit, in fact. Not in a horrible greedy attitude, but in a practical way so that we can continue to solve interesting, real-world problems for people.

Analytics help us measure how people use our app—not overall but the moment-to-moment interactions that make up workflows. Analytics let us validate the little things that make up the big things like entirely new features. Big things provide value to our customers and provide return on our investment. Breaking down the big things in your app as a flow of little things makes it easier to make decisions based on facts. Fact-based decision making carries more authority when you go to convince your stakeholders and tech team that you need their time and talent. If your organization has made decisions based on gut instinct and tradition, consider analytics as a new tool to help validate your choices.

Analytics, with respect to websites, have to do with collecting and reporting user interactions with pages hosted from your web server. The goal is finding trends in measuring how your customers are using and viewing your work to better enable them to use your technology.

Getting good feedback is tough. Once you make a product design decision, how do you know you made it correctly? What if a change went wrong? How would your users tell you? Maybe they blast you on Twitter or give you a one-star rating but do not list specifically what mistakes were made. Getting out of the office and meeting random people at coffee shops is a good way to get feedback because you can hear what they say, and better yet, watch what they do.

Jeff Gothelf recommends this as a starting point for educating your team:

> Collaborative discovery is an approach to research that gets the entire team out of the building—literally and figuratively—to meet with and learn from customers. It gives everyone on the team a chance to see how the hypotheses are testing and, most importantly, multiplies the number of inputs the team can use to gather customer insight.
>
> Jeff Gothelf with Josh Seiden, *Lean UX: Applying Lean Principles to Improve User Experience* (Sebastopol: O'Reilly Media, Inc., 2013, p. 74)

There are lots of good reasons to be inspired by his suggestion. It's surely worth trying to see if it becomes a part of your toolbox.

My challenge with that plan is wondering if it scales over time. Scheduling team outings into the field to accumulate user responses for frequent changes is time consuming. I'm also stuck visiting people only in my general region. I dream of one day having hundreds of thousands and possibly millions of users, and talking to a statistically significant number of them will be impossible.

Instead, I'll be better informed if I have a system through which I can sample all my users—no matter how many there are. Then I can truly learn what they like and don't like about my app more quickly and confidently. That's why anonymous analytics are crucial to my plan for building remarkable user experiences.

As soon as changes are made and deployed into the field, we start seeing waves of users telling us if we made good choices. Analytics let us know if things are clicked, pushed, tapped, and swiped more often or less. Looking at the data over hours, days, and weeks lets you know if changes were well received or poorly understood or simply didn't matter. From there, you can decide to take more actions. Engineers tasked with turning slow code into fast code know the first rule of Code Club is: Measure. If an engineer can't measure how slow a chunk of logic is, they're wasting their time making code changes because they won't know if things become better (faster) or worse (slower). Learning from that, we can say that changing user interfaces, experiences, contents, layouts, and responsive design ought to be tested.

Embrace change. So much of the startup culture is based around pivoting, A/B testing, optimizing signup conversion, and seeking market acceptance. Attributes for a modern company's new hire are surely based around these evocative, change-related subjects.

People can be skeptical of change because they're fearful of what they think it means. People can want assurance that an investment will pay off and demand all the answers before choosing to begin. People can have an attitude that they want to finish something and be done with it. Rarely is this level of control available to us, and that level of control is an illusion.

Are your changes to a mobile site better enabling your users to use your technology? While making design changes, ask yourself:

- Are call-to-action buttons more often hit when you make changes to your CSS breaking points specially made for a phone?

- Does turning a row of buttons into a drop-down menu for tablet form factors make users touch the options more readily?

- Does making images fluid to better scale down with smaller screens help or hurt your product sales pitch?

Turn to analytics to come up with answers to your questions. This might sound more like science than art to you, and I'll assure you there's nothing wrong with that.

If all of this sounds like too much math or is pushing you uncomfortably toward science, I encourage you to stay strong and see how you can internalize analytics to empower your creative process. Establishing a loop in which you keenly observe, propose educated guesses about how things are used, create a test in which you put changes into public action, and then measure the outcome sounds very much like the scientific method. It is, and that's perfectly fine. This describes the core loop of our modern scientific process, and it's well worth taking it for your own needs. I'm worried there's a split in our culture that pits art and science at opposite ends of a spectrum. What's worse to me is that they are characterized as being opposed to one another. It's a shame to me, wrong headed, and worst yet, not helpful. Scientists must dream, too, after all, and I think artists and designers will do well to postulate and evaluate.

For all creative leaders reading this book, I advise you to help your team merge some of these principles into their daily work. It will raise their level of quality by pushing their efforts past intuition and reference to what has worked in the past. These are helpful ways to start a collaborative conversation, but reality check that work with analytics. Measure how well solutions perform and either improve them or cut them, but try to remove the guesswork whenever possible.

In this chapter, I've chosen Google Analytics as the tool I want to show you how to use. It's one of the most popular systems because it has a complete set of features, it works on both websites and native apps, and it has a free tier that makes it easily within your reach right now.

ANALYTICS-DRIVEN DESIGN

How can analytics inform the decisions that artists and designers make? What specific numbers are the most helpful? Many are useful, but let's focus on a few specific examples and how they can better inform your choices during parts of the creative process. Given all possible options in the universe, how can some numbers guide you to a more successful conclusion?

Screen Sizes

Find out exactly what resolution customers' devices are presenting when they view your site. Discover the array of screen sizes and how often they happen during visits. If screen sizes are trending upward, trending downward, or holding steady, you can be more confident in the designs you're making by looking at these numbers. Keep track of screen resolutions and create new breakpoints in your responsive design to match popular form factors.

You might be surprised at the screen sizes reported for your website. What if they're bigger than you expected? Your audience could be made up of people viewing your website full screen on a high-end monitor. That too is something you want to know and respond to—you're probably not taking advantage of the full width of a display that big. Centering a block of content along a web page has been a good solution in the past, but a few inches of blank space along the left and right margins might look boring and need filling.

Device Brand and Name

If you find that your website is frequently visited mostly by Apple devices, be sure to feature iPhones and iPads in your documentation and illustrations. Allow your users to feel more welcome in your supporting material by showing the devices you know they're using. When designing advertising, drop screen shots of your website into the frames of Android devices if you see they're more popular. Determining exactly which hardware users visit on is surprisingly easy.

Know Your Audience

As you learn about analytics and what they do to validate you work and confirm your choices, require them in your projects. Some people believe demand for measuring user performance in an app or website inevitably comes from the business development group. What if your biz-dev folks don't know enough about analytics to appreciate them and ask for them? Then it's up to you to demand that analytics be planned and built into your websites and apps. Once the idea is built into your culture, you won't need to put much effort into asking for them. I predict everyone in your organization will want analytics once they see the concrete benefit.

DEVELOPER CHOICES THROUGH ANALYTICS

How can analytics inform the decisions developers make? An excellent use is finding out what operating system is most popular. If a new version of Android or iOS ships out with a hot new feature, you can track what percentage of your users have it on their mobile devices. Once you find the trend of use is moving upward and it hits some minimum threshold (say 20%) that makes it worth investing in the feature, you can be assured it is providing value to your users, and you ought to schedule time to implement it.

Along the same lines, track the versions of operating systems and watch as older ones start decreasing in appearance. Once a legacy operating system version drops below some threshold (say 5%) that makes it too expensive to maintain for the little use it gets, you can be assured it's worth cutting support for it. Don't bother fixing bugs in features nobody uses. Don't bother testing on an operating system nobody wants. There are always better ways to allocate your limited time. Lean into forward-thinking technologies that you know your users will soon move to. This is easy to see as you find trends on how quickly users have adopted new versions of their preferred operating systems. What category of users upgrades to the latest versions of their OS most quickly? Is it iOS or Android customers? Use the past to inform your future decisions.

PROJECT DECISION MAKING WITH ANALYTICS

How can analytics inform the decisions that project managers make? Management should lead a culture of analytics at their company. Setting an example for everyone on their team, a product owner will refer to analytics performance to set goals for success before project work begins and measure their effectiveness once the app is live and customer facing.

Before investing in a mobile-first redesign to an existing site, the project manager can first determine if mobile customers are already interested in visiting the website. Real-world mobile usage can inform whether this project gets prioritized.

Since managers are responsible for purchasing hardware for the team, they can check to see which devices are most often used. It doesn't make sense to have QA staff test on a device that your audience barely owns.

Engagement numbers show the dedication of customers. A product owner can find out if new customers are arriving through acquisition channels and whether legacy ones continue to return. Keep an eye on older devices that no longer come to the site. This helps budget limited resources, such as time and money, toward the modern and emerging devices, browsers, and operating systems. If usage is dropping to 5% or below, there's a decision to make. Take time to mindfully decide what to do with the support. Invest time and talent to grow it or invest to remove the underperforming feature.

WHAT IF YOU DON'T HAVE A RUNNING SITE WITH ANALYTICS?

Much of this chapter talks about drawing reports against historical data. You might be wondering what this means if you don't have a public site running analytics. How can you benefit? It's never too late to start recording analytics. If you already have a website in production, add analytics immediately. Start finding out if you're performing for your people.

If you're building a site from scratch and want to learn from analytics before sending out into the Internet, try teaming up with someone. In the computer programming world, this tactic is called "pair programming" or "pairing." It simply admits that an individual can't realistically know everything, and that's all right. It's nothing to worry over, so let's get past that while moving on to solving problems. I think pairing makes real the proverbial cliché that two heads are better than one. Historically we've called this collaborating, teaming up, and combining forces. Try looking around to find mature websites and web apps that have a profile similar to yours. Consider judging size, user persona, operating environment, production schedule, and any other characteristics that appear alike. Here are some informed sources from whom you can learn:

- If you're in a large company, look for a sister organization with a similar project already in use.

- If you're in a client-services group, perhaps a former customer will allow you access to their data from a site you've built for them.

- If you're in a city of any size, contact your wider professional network with links established from local meetups.

There are always alternatives when you need help. There are always people needing help who might reach out to you.

Adding Google Analytics to Your Site

I will introduce you to analytics by using Google's product. It's easily accessed and feature rich, and signing up for even the free tier gives you access to great capabilities. Later in this chapter, you'll read about alternative solutions, but for now, let's work on using this one.

Visit Google's product website and sign up:

```
http://www.google.com/analytics/
```

Their website guides you through the sign-up process as well as the first steps. Initially you'll want to:

1. Create an account representing your project, or company

2. Create a property representing an aspect of that account, such as a website

3. Planning ahead, you should create two different properties: development and production. The development version is for your team to use while building and testing. The production version is the final one your customers will use. You don't want your test data to get mixed with your real production data. Just remember to switch the analytics account code from development to production when you go live.

4. Copy the snippet of source code from the Google Analytics property page under a menu called ".JS Tracking Code." It's about 10 lines of JavaScript put on each page on your website that you want Google to know about and measure with analytics. This might be on the single index.html of an incredibly simple one-page website. For a multipage site, it must be put on every .html file you're building.

Once you've added this JavaScript to your web pages, they'll start reporting analytics data to Google.

READING THE GOOGLE ANALYTICS DEFAULT DASHBOARD

Once you have your website or web app reporting analytics through the Google SDK (software development kit) libraries, you'll start seeing data. A limited amount of data is reported in real time, but the bulk of it is accumulated in temporary storage and processed once a day, reducing the burden of crunching events into numbers. All the numbers are available, and you can crack open the data and peek around. Looking into the default dashboard is intimidating for more than a few hardy souls.

When I look at the dashboard with new teammates, there's no other way to describe the feeling. My friends and colleagues see all of the dozens of pages of reports, and they feel like a flood of big data is hosing them down. Can a person really drown in numbers? Mentally, you can. Historical collections in aggregate are reassuring, but for daily reference, we need to simplify our reporting process by dialing into what's necessary.

Necessary to whom? Self-interest dictates one person or a team is only interested in what they're interested in. Enjoying a highly targeted stream of analytics data is much better than trying to cope with a flood of big data.

Is there a way to limit data collections to only what we need? No, that would be a mistake, because sometime in the future, we might have new business needs and want to draw conclusions on historical data for new insights. The first rule of big data is saving our data, and if it's not there, we're stuck at a dead end. Instead we want filtered reporting, and Google Analytics has a fantastic way to do that. You can create a custom dashboard that dials in to the specific views you want to track and learn from. Custom dashboards are easily shared with your teammates who have access to the same projects you do. Hard work invested in handcrafting a custom dashboard is only done once for a team, because it's only a few clicks away from the entire group.

CRUCIAL DATA POINTS

We've already said that using the default dashboard provides access to all the analytics data our site collects, but its challenge is that it provides access to all the analytics data. I want our first exploration into analytics to be focused toward the first-class mobile-specific stats that best help you immediately.

1. Total Session Visits
2. Device Category
3. Screen Resolution
4. Mobile Screen Resolution
5. Mobile Device Branding
6. Mobile Device Model
7. Visitor Country/Territory
8. Browser Name
9. Operating System
10. Android Operating System Version
11. iOS Version

Use these daily to get started in analytics reporting and assessment. Once you feel smart and confident using the reports from this list, take time to pull in new and interesting-looking ones. In the next section, you will see how to create a custom dashboard dedicated to mobile devices. What it reports tells you how to better build responsive designs.

Analytics have a real-time section that shows you information about your users as the usage happens. What this section reports is limited because it's relatively complex for the system to receive these data, process them, and put them into a form that can be reported. All data are stored and processed in bulk once or twice a day. I think of it as overnight to keep it simple.

Crafting a Custom Reporting Dashboard

In the previous section, a list of 11 stats was highlighted as especially valuable for hammering responsive web design into shape. Let's work through building a custom-made reporting dashboard that looks like this:

Here's how we create a custom reporting dashboard fine-tuned for your needs:

1.   Log into Google Analytics

2.   Choose your website's property name from your account's list. For example, on mine, I click on my blog website, which is enabled with analytics.

3.   You'll land on a default view of your site's information that probably shows an audience overview report. Click on the "Dashboards" option on the left-hand list to open it up and show its actions.

4.   Select the menu option called "+ New Dashboard"

5. A dialog box will pop up titled "Create dashboard" with "Blank Canvas" selected by default, which is what we want. Here is a chance to name your dashboard. You might want to call it "Responsive Analytics Reporting." Press "Create Dashboard" when you're ready.

Create dashboard   ✕

Blank Canvas	Starter Dashboard

| Responsive Analytics Reporting| | **Create Dashboard** | **Import from Gallery** | Cancel |

6. A dialog box will pop up titled "Add a Widget," prompting you to add the first reporting element. Let's create the first one on our list.
    - Title it "Total Session Visits"
    - Select the "2.1 Metric" option under the Standard group
    - Under the "show the following metric" option, click on the "Add a metric" input to search for the "Sessions" entry on the drop-down list
    - Press the Save button, and you're done with your first reporting widget
    - You'll look to it to learn how many users have viewed your site.

Add a Widget   ✕

Widget title:

Sessions

Standard:

2.1 METRIC	TIMELINE	GEOMAP	TABLE	PIE	BAR

Real-time:

2.1 COUNTER	TIMELINE	GEOMAP	TABLE

Show the following metric:

Sessions   ▾

Filter this data:

Add a filter

Link to Report or URL:

Save   Cancel   Clone widget

7. Click the toolbar option called "+ Add Widget" to show the same dialog box you just used, and we'll add another reporting widget.

- Title it "Visits by Device Category"
- Select the "Table" option under the standard group
- Under the "Display the following columns" section, click "Add a dimension" and choose "Device Category"
- Click "Add a metric" and choose "Sessions" from the list
- Press the "Save" button and you're done
- You'll look to this list to see what category of device users viewed your website with. This includes desktop, mobile, and tablet.

8.   Click "Add a Widget" to show the dialog box for adding another reporting widget.
- Title it "Screen Resolutions"
- Select the "Table" option under the standard group
- Under the "Display the following columns" section, click on "Add a dimension" and choose "Screen Resolution"
- Click on "Add a metric" and choose "Sessions" from the list
- Press the Save button and you're done
- You'll look to this list to view the top 10 screen resolutions that view your website. Desktop and handheld are combined here.

Add a Widget   ✕

Widget title:

Screen Resolutions

Standard:

2.1 METRIC	TIMELINE	GEOMAP	TABLE	PIE	BAR

Real-time:

2.1 COUNTER	TIMELINE	GEOMAP	TABLE

Display the following columns:

Screen Resolution ▾   ↓   Sessions ▾   ↓   Add a metric ▾ ⊗

Show a table with 10 rows ⇕

Filter this data:

Add a filter

Link to Report or URL: 🗒

Save   Cancel   Clone widget

9. Click "Add a Widget" to show the dialog box for adding another reporting widget.
- Title it "Mobile Screen Resolutions"
- Select the "Table" option under the standard group
- Under the "Display the following columns" section, click on "Add a dimension" and choose "Screen Resolution"
- Click "Add a metric" and choose "Sessions" from the list
- Under "Filter this data," click on "Add a filter"
- The first item defaults to "Only show"; change it to "Don't show"
- Click on "Add a dimension" and set it to "Device Category" from the dropdown list
- The second item on this row defaults to "Containing"—leave that, but type "desktop" into the adjacent input field.
- Press the "Save" button and you're done
- You'll look to this list to see the top 10 screen resolutions that view your website that are only from mobile and tablet, because desktop answers are excluded

Add a Widget   ✕

Widget title:

Mobile Screen Resolutions

Standard:

2.1 METRIC	TIMELINE	GEOMAP	TABLE	PIE	BAR

Real-time:

2.1 COUNTER	TIMELINE	GEOMAP	TABLE

Display the following columns:

Screen Resolution   ↓   Sessions   ↓   Add a metric

Show a table with 10 rows

Filter this data:

Don't show   Device Category   Containing   desktop

Add a filter

Link to Report or URL:

Save   Cancel   Clone widget

10. Click on "Add a Widget" to show the dialog box for adding another reporting widget.

- Title it "Mobile Device Branding"
- Select the "Table" option under the standard group
- Under the "Display the following columns" section, click on "Add a dimension" and choose "Mobile Device Branding"
- Click "Add a metric" and choose "Sessions" from the list
- Press the "Save" button and you're done
- You'll look to this list to view the top company names that make mobile devices popular for viewing your website.

11. Click on "Add a Widget" to show the dialog box for adding another reporting widget.
- Title it "Mobile Device Model"
- Select the "Table" option under the standard group
- Under the "Display the following columns" section, click on "Add a dimension" and choose "Mobile Device Model"
- Click on "Add a metric" and choose "Sessions" from the list
- Press the "Save" button and you're done
- You'll look to this list to see the top company names that make mobile devices popular for viewing your website.

12.   Click on "Add a Widget" to show the dialog box for adding another reporting widget.

- Title it "Visits by Country"
- Select the "Table" option under the standard group
- Under the "Display the following columns" section, click on "Add a dimension" and choose "Country/Territory"
- Click on "Add a metric" and choose "Sessions" from the list
- Press the "Save" button and you're done
- You'll look to this list to find the top countries visiting your website.

13.   Click on "Add a Widget" to show the dialog box for adding another reporting widget.
- Title it "Browser Popularity"
- Select the "Table" option under the standard group
- Under the "Display the following columns" section, click on "Add a dimension" and choose "Browser"
- Click "Add a metric" and choose "Sessions" from the list
- Press the "Save" button and you're done
- You'll look to this list to see the most popular browsers that your customers use to view your website.

Widget Settings   ✕

Widget title:

Browser Popularity

Standard:

2.1 METRIC	TIMELINE	GEOMAP	TABLE	PIE	BAR

Real-time:

2.1 COUNTER	TIMELINE	GEOMAP	TABLE

Display the following columns:

Browser ▾ ↓ Sessions ▾ ↓ **Add a metric** ▾ ⊗

Show a table with [10 rows ↕]

Filter this data:

Add a filter

Link to Report or URL:

[   ]

Save Cancel   Clone widget   Delete widget

14. Click on "Add a Widget" to show the dialog box for adding another reporting widget.

- Title it "O/S Platform"
- Select the "Table" option under the standard group
- Under the "Display the following columns" section, click on "Add a dimension" and choose "Operating System"
- Click "Add a metric" and choose "Sessions" from the list
- Press the "Save" button and you're done
- You'll look to this list to see the most popular operating systems that run devices viewing your website. Desktop and handheld are combined here.

15. Click on "Add a Widget" to show the dialog box for adding another reporting widget.

- Title it "iOS Version"
- Select the "Table" option under the standard group
- Under the "Display the following columns" section, click on "Add a dimension" and choose "Operating System Version"
- Click on "Add a metric" and choose "Sessions" from the list
- Under "Filter this data," click on "Add a filter"
- The first item defaults to "Only show"—leave it at that
- Click on "Add a dimension" and set it to "Operating System" from the drop-down list
- The second item on this row defaults to "Containing"—leave it at that and type "iOS" in the adjacent input field
- Press the "Save" button and you're done
- You'll look to this list to see the specific versions of the iOS operating system running Apple-made handhelds.

16. Click on "Add a Widget" to show the dialog box for adding another reporting widget.

- Title it "Android Version"
- Select the "Table" option under the standard group
- Under the "Display the following columns" section, click on "Add a dimension" and choose "Operating System Version"
- Click "Add a metric" and choose "Sessions" from the list
- Under "Filter this data," click on "Add a filter"
- The first item defaults to "Only show"—leave it at that
- Click on "Add a dimension" and set it to "Operating System" from the dropdown list
- The second item on this row defaults to "Containing"—leave it at that and type "Android" in the adjacent input field
- Press the "Save" button and you're done
- You'll look to this list to see the specific versions of the Android operating system running on its handhelds.

17.   Now that you've established your reporting widgets, take a few moments to marvel at your creation. It gives a nice, high-level overview of how your website is serving your customers. Finalize a few dashboard-level settings. For example, click on the toolbar option "Customize Dashboard" and choose your preferred layout. I suggest a four-column mode to allow all of the widgets a chance to display at once. You'll also notice that you can drag and drop reporting widgets around the dashboard space to group them in ways that make the most sense to you.

Your dashboard will look something like this.

It's time to pause and celebrate. This is next-level stuff.

CONFIRMING AND DEBUGGING ANALYTICS ON YOUR SITE

As a product engineer, I want my programs to work, but I don't always get what I want. It's nice to want things, but I'm in the business of delivering reliable, functional, simple software. Often I'm in a cycle of testing, diagnosing, fixing, and confirming my code as much as I'm writing it. Thinking about that, I offer to you two ways of testing and ensuring your analytics is working.

First, Google Analytics has a reporting section called "Real-Time," and I devote a lot of hours to looking at it. When I suggested earlier that you create a specific project devoted to your team during development, this is the payoff. Because you'll have a small group of people running the website during work in your office, you can look at the real-time reporting to see how your actions on the website are affecting data recording. You'll see only a handful of analytics measurements are reported in real time. That's on purpose.

Second, Google provides a plugin to its Chrome web browser. Search for "Google Analytics Debugger Chrome plugin" to find it in their online store. Download it and install it to your browser to reveal a switch for you to turn on for debugging insights. It reports an audit trail of what analytics are reporting from you website by printing out information in the console window of the browser's developer tools.

Event tracking, an advanced topic covered in what follows, can be complicated for you to code and test, but this tool helps make confirmation easier. Product managers can use it to interactively probe what's reported as they use the website.

To see the console output, start with opening the developer tools in the Chrome browser:

- Click on the "View" toolbar item
- Click on the "Developer" menu item
- Click on the "JavaScript Console" submenu item

Exploring Advanced Topics

What we have reviewed here is just an introduction to analytics. You'll want to invest weeks understanding them. As you gain more experience and confidence using analytics to measure your mobile viewers, you'll start wanting more advanced features. Consider adding one of these to your workflow where it makes sense.

EVENT TRACKING

At first, it might seem that Google Analytics will only track page views, but it can also track events. A user event is any interaction with the webpage—hovering or tapping any interface elements. What if you have a web app—a single-page application continually replacing the contents of its single page? Page views aren't really helpful here, since you only have one page. Attach an event to everything your user can tap, flip, swipe, and set. Tracking events lets you measure whether the things you design and build are actually used by people. If they're not used, invest time to make them better or invest money to remove them.

TRANSACTIONS

E-commerce transactions let you put a monetary value to all of those events and page flows. Naturally, e-commerce gives you a chance to report revenue earned from outright purchases. Then it's an easy matter to report through a dashboard how much an event is worth based on how much it's used and the base value you assign to it. If something on your site isn't performing to your needs, find out about it and make it better or remove it.

FUNNELS

Funnel conversions are a favorite of mine. They allow you to define a series of steps a user takes from page to page. For example, a store would want to know how many steps it takes the user to browse, add, and check out. Let analytics tell you how your site performs when it comes to selling products. Sales aren't the only reason to do this. Imagine connecting the dots along a path to change a setting. Do people start eagerly and then stop somewhere before completion? Let analytics reporting tell you where exactly the dropoff occurs as all people start at the top of a funnel and slide down it.

If there's an obvious dropoff in the steps, put your best people on making that step easier, clearer, whatever. Then see if your changes work. If they enable more of your customers to pass through the funnel, see if they come out the exit end successfully. The funnel starts big at the entrance and progressively tightens as the steps progress. It's accepted that not everyone will come through the end, but it's an important goal to ensure enough do to make your investment worthwhile for running your business.

As you learn more about Google Analytics and internalize how to bring this tool to your craft, you'll discover even more advanced techniques. The field of analytics is relatively young, but its history is already varied, full, and exciting.

Alternatives

It's always important to constantly judge our tools. When a real-world hammer cracks or a metal chisel bends, it's easy to loosely hold it in your hand and casually say, "It's all busted—let's go get a new one." Digital tools aren't so easily judged, are they? They'll never break so obviously, but they will show wear and age. Then we need to make a choice. Sometimes we replace them with the newer model and upgrade. Sometimes we need to research alternatives. We must pick them up and test them out in real-world situations. Then we really know if the tool is fit for the purpose. Here is a brief list of noticeable alternatives to Google Analytics: Kissmetrics, Piwik, ChartBeat, Mint, Clicky, MixPanel, and gaug.es. This is a relatively crowded market, with many alternatives for every budget and need. Check it all out and make your final choices.

Fact-Based Decisions for Effective Design

Most people are attracted to or at least curious about the big-data phenomenon. It seems like something that's only in the domain of different teams at other companies. Journalists writing on the subject herald big data as the next wave of computer science that will help every industry imaginable, but without concrete examples of what it means, does, or amounts to. This phrase appears weekly in the industry press in one form or another. For me, analytics strikes at the heart of big data. It's your website being measured, collected, and reported in the context of your users viewing it and applying it to their lives. Facts about your website are accumulated daily and without pause as blocks of numbers.

When looking at analytics, I don't simply see numbers anymore. A while back, I realized the truth—that these numbers are our users' voices. We must listen to them as they communicate with us through analytics.

The lean startup and user experience (UX) movement proclaims that designers must get out of the office and venture out into the real world to show apps and sites to real people. Encouraging normal people to use work in progress is the only way to find out if assumptions about user interface are correctly producing positive experiences. While I surely believe this as a maker, I doubt its long-term validity as an engineer.

We engineers think of our software running on one server but then two, four, and more. As the business gains customers and success, we consider how our services can rise to meet the demand. This is "scaling." We ask ourselves if we build software that scales up over time reliably, sometimes routinely, occasionally rapidly, without drama to meet increasing demand. Given that point of view, I think the idea of getting out of the office to meet our customers and seek their approval is a tactic that helps validate and build confidence early but does not scale over time. As our software is loaded up on the public Internet, we cannot possibly go out to meet new users across the world and cannot possibly understand who all of them are. Analytics help us do that as a proxy that meets our users where they are. No matter who they are, what devices they use, which time zones they operate in, or where they live, analytics tirelessly listen to them, record their actions, and let us graph figures from those statistics.

As you take recorded events and report on them, you'll draw out factual understanding from your users' raw data. Comparing reports from quarterly data ranges, weekly, even daily, you'll see trends emerge. Although various industries warn against the volatile nature of predicting the future, the accepted practice is that past trends indicate future actions. Anticipate what your customers need and move toward them letting them better use your work.

- Are screens getting smaller or larger?
- Are operating systems fading away or growing in popularity?
- Are new geographical regions showing up?

- Are marketing and product investments paying off by acquiring new customers and adding revenue?

- Are people engaging with your content when they arrive and sticking around as long as you want them to?

- Are new users finding your site and are legacy ones returning?

- Are buttons and UI options easily understood and valuable enough to use?

Getting out of the office and directly asking some of your prospective users if new designs make sense is crucial for early critiques. Mixing in analytics will help you gain understanding of how sites in production perform at a large scale. Believe me, I'm not trying to take the fun out of the creative workflow by adding in so many numbers. Analytics are tools like any other, and they have their place. It's a new enough field, however, that I must hold it up to the light and let you have a good look at it. Intuition is always a valid jumping-off point for creative endeavors, but if we want to support a business through making money, please take time to investigate how measuring and reporting will support your professional efforts.

CHAPTER 11

Responsive Screen-Capture Project

Let's Build Something Cool

The point of this chapter is reaching up into the open-source world and pulling down a tool called PhantomJS. Incorporating it into your toolbox will take a steady hand. It has unique applications for critiquing, testing, and documenting your websites.

Fundamentally, PhantomJS is a web browser that doesn't show you what it's looking at. You drive it on the command line, and it reports on what you ask it about. Questions are formed via small JavaScript scripts.

Some of this is going to seem advanced, and it's going to involve installing tools and writing code. It's all right, though. Hang in there and keep up with the explanations, because it's worth it. By the time we're done, you're going to have a useful creation that helps you in ways I can't predict. It's going to open up your ideas of what's possible and power up your thinking for changes to this system and new inventions into the future.

BUILD A CUSTOMIZED TOOL CHAIN

There's an idea of a tool chain. Computers are good at running a tool, taking its output, and directing it into another one. Chaining tools together by redirecting one's output into the next one's input is theoretically endless, and the computer makes it possible. Remixing your original data through a custom tool chain creates super-interesting outcomes.

Assembling this specific tool chain is something of a green-field project. There are no real constraints from previous work or required demands. Restrictions only come from our own

Tool Chain

Connecting inputs to outputs for final creation

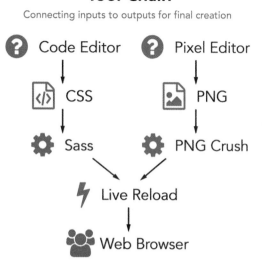

imaginations. While we stay optimistic, we can dream it, plan it, and build it into being. No need to let little glitches turn into big worries, because everything can be figured out over time. Much of being an engineer is believing that something can ·be done. Otherwise I wouldn't show up to work each day, because work is just too complicated to think about continuing. Have a strong heart and keep moving forward. There's always another way!

WHY PROGRAMMERS USE COMMAND-LINE TOOLS

Why does it seem like engineers and programmers like command-line tools? What is it about the text-only interface of a Terminal window or a DOS prompt that makes them satisfied? Happy even?

Thirty years ago, the creators of the UNIX operating system articulated a set of beliefs around how programs should work, and that has influenced the way programmers have built software tools ever since. Really, it's how we see the world. Each program is made to solve a single, small problem very well. You can solve bigger problems by chaining these small utilities together. By making the output of one the input into another, you can combine them. Any complex machine, like an automobile engine, is made up of individual pieces operating together in perfect union.

Command-line tools are functional, reliable, and simple. Simplicity is a key design decision, because writing one of these things means you can start and finish it. No need for feature creep, tacking on more and more abilities over time. A command-line tool's usability is defined by how well it plays with other tools.

It's an assembly-line process. Success comes from the fact that computer systems are excellent at following a clearly written, step-by-step process over and over again. It's the heart of what makes writing a computer program possible. Human beings think they're good at following directions, but when a process must be done repeatedly, they get bored, and boredom leads to mistakes. Computers never get bored; they excel at routine.

PhantomJS

PhantomJS is an open-source project built and maintained by a team of volunteers. It's a command-line tool, naturally, but what's special about it is that it's a fully functional web browser without a user interface. Surely that sounds unusual. Browsers are built to allow people to read well-designed pages full of beautifully rendered graphics and useful prose.

When run on a command line, PhantomJS doesn't show a single pixel of a page—it's a headless browser. I'll explain why you would want this later. Just believe me, even though the page is unseen, it exists virtually in the tool's memory.

PhantomJS offers a few ways of getting at that unseen page sitting in its imagination via some lightweight programming. Some code is necessary, but it's brief, and it's easier to understand once we get into the real practical use if it. Coding is done in JavaScript, which is great, because it's a daily-use tool for you given its popularity on the web. Any chance of writing some code is a good thing. I feel like it's always worth getting better at the core languages of the web. Every exercise we complete improves our mastery of our craft.

> Why is PhantomJS called headless? Today, computers are things in front of us. Laptops, phones, and tablets are our personal computers. In the beginning, they were huge contraptions behind locked doors. The way programmers interacted with them was through a keyboard-and-monitor set tethered to the mainframe via a network connection. This setup was called a head. PhantomJS doesn't need a monitor or observer for its results to work perfectly fine.

HEADLESS WEBSITE TESTING

PhantomJS is great for testing that a website is behaving the way you expect it to. Engineers can write small scripts that simulate user interaction and check that everything responds as it should. PhantomJS reads your script and plays back all the user interactions for you in the virtual page. We gain confidence in our work by testing it in this way, because anytime we make a change, we can just run our PhantomJS script to confirm that nothing broke. The more tests, the stronger the confidence.

If you want to take testing to the next level, you could integrate a testing framework—such as Jasmine, Mocha, or QUnit—to help set up the conditions for the test, compare results against expected ones, and report how many of the tests succeeded and failed.

NETWORK MONITORING

Building websites that quickly respond to their users is crucial. As an engineer, I'm very interested in knowing more about performance, optimization, and scaling as more people show up to have a look at my websites. Building a tool that uses PhantomJS to load a popular page while measuring how long it takes to load is a fantastic thing. Because it's driven on the command line, I can automate this process. Then I could launch it morning, noon, and night every day of the week to see if my site is slower at any particular time. I can record how long every resource takes to load, seeking culprits for holding up page rendering. As a record of results grows over time, trends reveal how my site's speed is doing and whether certain resources are taking too long to stream across the network from server to browser.

SCREEN SHOTS

PhantomJS can take a screen shot of your website, so we can automate the process of taking screen shots. Why would we want to do that? There are lots of good reasons you'll find useful, and we'll review those soon. First, we'll install PhantomJS, and then we'll write a little bit of JavaScript to control it from the command line. The way it generates a page image is by using the WebKit rendering engine, and that is some of the technology historically used by Chrome and Safari.

INSTALLING PHANTOMJS

You'll want to install PhantomJS once you've read through this chapter and decided that it's a powerful tool to add to your professional toolbox. Please look to the download page on the official website for instructions on installing PhantomJS:

```
http://phantomjs.org/download.html
```

I believe the information you'll read there is clearly written and current. There's no need for this book to duplicate that effort. On that page, you'll find information regarding downloading and installing this tool on both Windows and OS X.

Designers and developers on OS X have an alternative choice. It's one that I use and want to highlight. Opening a Terminal window and issuing the command `brew install phantomjs` is another way of installing PhantomJS. "Brew" is short for Homebrew, a package manager. Engineers have the idea of making app installs, updates, and deletions easier. Once again, it's on the command line, and I advise you not to let it intimidate you. I recommend embracing the command line at your own pace and letting it add value to your creative workflow. Instructions on how to install Homebrew are available at `http://brew.sh/`.

BEGINNING WAY OF USING PHANTOMJS

We're going to write a brief program that uses PhantomJS for taking a screen shot of a website saved to a file.

PhantomJS installed on your development environment is like a miniature shiny robot awaiting your orders. It's time to make it do your bidding. For that, we'll need to write a brief JavaScript program that feeds it commands to follow. Much of the JavaScript is simply assigning useful values to a collection of well-named variables, accessing the PhantomJS module, and calling a couple of its functions. In principle, it's straightforward yet powerful.

In a source-code text editor or IDE of your choice, enter the following JavaScript code and save it out to a work folder where you keep your experimental tools. Save it with the filename `SimplePageScreenShot.js`.

```javascript
var URL = 'http://www.threethumbisland.com/';
var WIDTH = 1024;
var HEIGHT = 2048;

var webPage = require('webpage');
var page = webPage.create();
var fileName = '3thumb' + '_' + WIDTH + '_' +
   HEIGHT + '.png';

page.viewportSize = {width: WIDTH, height: HEIGHT};
page.open(URL, function(status) {
   if (status === 'success') {
      page.render(fileName);
      console.log('Successfully saved web page screenshot.');
   } else {
      console.log('Could not open page.');
   }
   phantom.exit();
});
```

Running this app ought to be a simple matter of:

1. From the command line, change directory into the folder in which you have saved the program

2. Enter the command `phantomjs SimplePageScreenShot.js` and wait a few seconds for it to work

3.   You'll find a newly created image file called `3thumb_1024_2048.png`. Feel free to open it in your favorite viewer and have a look

Let's review what the code does to ensure it makes sense to you. As we conduct the code reading, you'll see obvious places where you can change it and learn what it can do.

These lines in the program set up three basic configuration options for telling PhantomJS what makes up our image. The variable names are descriptive enough to be self-commenting. `URL` is the website you want to have a picture of, and this can be your work-in-progress website running on localhost. The `WIDTH` and `HEIGHT` are, of course, the pixel size of the imaginary browser window viewing this website. Note that PhantomJS will respect the width configuration but will in fact use whatever height is necessary to fit the page's content. We'll consider that a benefit for now, but I will also show you a way to cut that with authority in our next section. These are good variables to play with as you experiment with this brief program.

```
var URL = 'http://www.threethumbisland.com/';
var WIDTH = 1024;
var HEIGHT = 2048;
```

This section reaches for a library called webpage, requiring it into our program by a module name and assigning it to a variable for use later. This library of code comes bundled with PhantomJS. Next, a page object is created. We calculate a filename for the snapshot image file based on a few well-known variables. It's a relatively unique pattern that makes sense, but change it as you like.

```
var webPage = require('webpage');
var page = webPage.create();
var fileName = '3thumb' + '_' + WIDTH + '_' +
   HEIGHT + '.png';
```

This uses the PhantomJS page object to tell how big we want the virtual page rendered. We access a function on the page object called open, giving it the website URL that we want it to reference and a function that's run once the webpage is fully rendered. This is known as a callback function, and it is a key bit of why JavaScript is powerful. Libraries can be called, we let them go off and work for as long as they need to, and then they come back to our program when they're complete and have results for us to act upon.

```
page.viewportSize = {width: WIDTH, height: HEIGHT};
page.open(URL, function(status) {
```

Here, the PhantomJS comes back to our program through the callback function, having passed it an argument called status. Checking status is important for knowing if the website was rendered correctly. We check the value in the status variable against what we know the documentation tells us. Expect that PhantomJS sends in the word "success" if things are good and it has a page drawn in its imaginary browser. If that's true, we tell the page to save itself out to a file given the filename we came up with already.

To improve the user experience a little, we provide friendly feedback, printing a simple success message out to the command-line window.

```javascript
if (status === 'success') {
    page.render(fileName);
    console.log('Successfully saved web page screenshot.');
```

If the status variable doesn't have the word "success" in it, we know PhantomJS failed to generate a webpage in its memory. We don't exactly know why, but we'll trust the result and print a message telling our user something went wrong. That way they can try it again in case of a random network glitch or reread the source code to inspect it for a defect. Could have been a typo when writing the JavaScript.

```javascript
} else {
    console.log('Could not open page.');
}
```

Either way, we need to tell PhantomJS to clean up after itself by calling the exit function. Then our program naturally comes to an end.

```javascript
    phantom.exit();
});
```

That's all rather exciting, isn't it? Spend some time reading through the code to ensure you know what's happening. Change the URL, WIDTH, and HEIGHT variables to other websites at different devices sizes. Watch how this changes the program's behavior.

If you want to take a quick look at the PhantomJS programming documentation, have a look at this page, for example. It shows how to use some of the functions shown in the example computer program.

```
http://phantomjs.org/api/webpage/method/render.html
```

This website documents the overall PhantomJS API, and the URL details the render function in particular. An interesting thing you'll see listed is how many other file formats are available. I choose PNG because it has space-saving compression without any loss of quality. Have a look at the API reference and find out what other files you can use. Give them a quick try if you like to gain extra experience.

> API is an acronym for application programming interface. APIs have changed over time, but fundamentally, they are a way for a third party to offer up a bundle of code to serve our needs. Ultimately, it's a library with a well-documented way of talking to it.

POLISHING PASS?

How can we improve this program? Lots of ways. For example, the width, height, and URL are all fixed in place with hard-coded values. That means the program will do the exact same thing every time we run it. Changing its behavior means changing lines of code in an editor. That might be fine for the program author, but it's too inflexible to be a friendly experience for another user, especially one not as technical as we are. Hard-coding values defeats the eventual goal of crafting automation tools. In the next section, we'll improve upon this program, extending it and making it a more generally useful tool.

INTERMEDIATE WAY OF USING PHANTOMJS SCREEN SHOTS

Let's build on the previous `SimplePageScreenShot.js` program to improve it for flexibility. We'll have it look for command-line arguments that a user can tell it width, height, URL, and filename prefix. All the things that were hard coded before can now be changed every time it's run. This makes it more useful for you and your teammates and opens it up for future automation scripts.

In a source-code text editor, or IDE, of your choice, enter the following JavaScript code and save it out to a work folder in which you keep your experimental tools. Save it with the filename `WebPageScreenShot.js`.

```
var webPage = require('webpage');
var system = require('system');

var width, height, url, filePrefix;
var page, fileName;
```

```
if (system.args.length >= 5) {
  width = parseInt(system.args[1], 10);
  height = parseInt(system.args[2], 10);
  url = system.args[3];
  filePrefix = system.args[4];
  fileName = filePrefix + '_' + width + '_' +
    height + '.png';

  page = webPage.create();
  page.viewportSize = {width: width, height: height};
  page.clipRect = {top: 0, left: 0,
    width: width, height: height};

  page.open(url, function(status) {
    if (status === 'success') {
      page.render(fileName);
      console.log('Successfully saved screenshot to [' +
        fileName + ']');
    } else {
      console.log('Could not open page.');
    }
    phantom.exit();
  });
} else {
  console.log('like this: phantomjs WebPageScreenShot width height url
filenamePrefix');
      phantom.exit();
}
```

Running this app ought to be a simple matter of:

1.   From the command line, change directory into the folder in which you have saved
      the program

2.   Enter the command `phantomjs WebPageScreenShot.js 1280 1024 http://www.`
      `threethumbisland.com 3thumb` and wait a few seconds for it to work

3.   You'll find a newly created image file called `3thumb_1280_1024.png`. Feel free to open it in your favorite viewer and have a look

Let's review what the code does to ensure it makes sense to you. As we conduct the code reading, you'll see obvious places where you can change it to fit your needs.

These lines reach out for the PhantomJS webpage library by requiring it into your program by a module name. Another helper module is brought in from the basic NodeJS system libraries. Both are assigned to variables for use later.

```
var webPage = require('webpage');
var system = require('system');
```

Several variables are declared and given obvious names that clearly communicate a useful idea to the reader.

```
var width, height, url, filePrefix;
var page, fileName;
```

Our program expects four specific user inputs. Command-line tools refer to these as arguments. Using the system module lets us look at its `args` attribute and see that it holds an array of arguments passed into the program. We access that array's length attribute ensuring it has at least five entries.

```
if (system.args.length >= 5) {
```

If we expect four arguments, why check the array for five entries? Because PhantomJS always inserts the running program filename as the first entry. How do I know that? Admittedly, I expect that to happen given what I know as an engineer who has built command-line tools in other languages. Better than that is documentation:

```
http://phantomjs.org/api/system/property/args.html
```

Given that there are enough arguments passed to our program, we pull them out and store them so they're prepared for use. It seems like the `system.args` is already a variable that stores these user options. Must we store each of these in our own variables? No. I recommend it as a code style because it makes the program easier for a reader to understand. Assigning the value of strangely named `system.args[1]` into one named width suddenly reveals much meaning for future maintainers. Sometimes that's overworked and tired future you or another teammate once you've left the company. The function `parseInt` turns the command-line argument from a text string into a number.

```
if (system.args.length >= 5) {
    width = parseInt(system.args[1], 10);
    height = parseInt(system.args[2], 10);
    url = system.args[3];
    filePrefix = system.args[4];
    fileName = filePrefix + '_' + width + '_' +
        height + '.png';
```

We use the PhantomJS webpage module to create a page object. Then we tell it how big we want the virtual page rendered. The `clipRect` attribute is new and interesting. Using it, we tell PhantomJS to physically cut the virtually rendered page down to size. If we didn't, PhantomJS would let the height go as long as the website delivers content to view.

We access a function on the page object called open and give it the website URL we want it to reference and a function that's run once the webpage is fully rendered. This is known as a callback function, and it is a key bit of why JavaScript is powerful. Libraries can be called, we let them go off and work for as long as they need to, and then they come back to our program when they're complete and have results for us to act upon.

```
page = webPage.create();
page.viewportSize = {width: width, height: height};
page.clipRect = {top: 0, left: 0,
    width: width, height: height};


page.open(url, function(status) {
```

Here the PhantomJS comes back to our program through the callback function, having passed it an argument called status. Checking status is important for showing if the website was rendered correctly. We check the value in the status variable against what we know the documentation tells us. Expect that PhantomJS sends in the word "success" if things are good and it has a page drawn in its imaginary browser. If that's true, we tell the page to save itself out to a file given the filename we came up with already.

As friendly feedback, we print out to the terminal window a simple text prompt. It's not a GUI by any stretch of the imagination, but it helps improve the user experience in the reliable way that we can.

```
if (status === 'success') {
    page.render(fileName);
    console.log('Successfully saved screenshot to [' +
        fileName + ']');
```

If the status variable doesn't have the word "success" in it, we know PhantomJS failed to generate a webpage in its memory. We don't exactly know why, but we'll trust the result and print out a text prompt that tells our user something went wrong. That way they can try it again in case of a random network glitch or reread the source code and inspect it for a defect. Could have been a typo when writing the JavaScript.

```
} else {
    console.log('Could not open page.');
}
```

No matter if the webpage opening was a success or failure, we need to clean up after ourselves, telling PhantomJS we're done with it by calling its exit function. Then our program naturally comes to an end.

```
    phantom.exit();
});
```

This is the matching "else" to the logic checking if five command-line arguments are passed into the program. When too few or too many are found, we simple write a reminder to our users that tells them what they must do to get the program to work properly.

```
} else {
  console.log('like this: phantomjs WebPageScreenShot width height url
filenamePrefix');
  phantom.exit();
}
```

This is a solid improvement to the `SimplePageScreenShot.js` program introduced in the previous section. Try running it a few different ways, testing the logic and checking if enough arguments are given. Test various websites with various widths and heights that match handheld devices you know. See how the saved pictures render and respond to the sizes you give.

POLISHING PASS?

Can this program be improved? Yes, of course. Every creative work can be polished. One thing that comes to mind is checking if the command-line arguments sent into it are valid. User input can't be trusted. Good people make simple mistakes, and bad people conduct malicious attacks. All user input ought to be validated before use. For example:

- Are the width and height arguments actually numbers? Are they zero, negative, or outrageously large?

- Is the URL argument formatted the way a URL ought to be?

- Is the filename prefix a valid string that our operating system allows for a filename? What if someone sends in emoji characters?

ADVANCED WAY OF USING PHANTOMJS

Now that we've written code that enables us to take a screen shot of a website with pre-defined settings and rewritten it to dynamically let our user choose what they want, let's iterate and improve. Let's write a little program that calls our dynamic `WebPageScreenShot.JS` several times with an array of command-line arguments. Let's automate this process to take several pictures at once.

In a source-code text editor, or IDE, of your choice, enter the following JavaScript code and save it out to a work folder in which you keep your experimental tools. Save it with the filename `MultiShot.js`.

```
var TARGETS = [{
    url: 'http://www.threethumbisland.com',
    width: 1280,
    height: 1280,
```

```
      fileName: '3Thumb'
    }, {
      url: 'http://www.threethumbisland.com',
      width: 1024,
      height: 1280,
      fileName: '3Thumb'
    }, {
      url: 'http://www.threethumbisland.com',
      width: 768,
      height: 1280,
      fileName: '3Thumb'
    }, {
      url: 'http://www.threethumbisland.com',
      width: 320,
      height: 1280,
      fileName: '3Thumb'
    }];

var spawn = require('child_process').spawn;
var numFinished = 0;

TARGETS.forEach(function shootTarget(target, index, array) {

  var child;

  child = spawn('phantomjs', ['WebPageScreenShot.js',
    target.width, target.height, target.url,
    target.fileName]);

  child.stdout.on('data', function (data) {
    console.log(data);

  });
  child.on('exit', function () {
    numFinished += 1;
    if (numFinished === TARGETS.length) {
      phantom.exit(0);
    }
  });
});
```

Running this app ought to be a simple matter of:

1. From the command line, change directory into the folder in which you saved the program

2. Enter the command `phantomjs MultiShot.js` and wait a few seconds for it to work

3. You'll find four newly created image files starting with `3thumb` in their names. Feel free to open any of them in your favorite viewer and have a look. You'll see a list like this:

Let's review what the code does to ensure it makes sense to you. As we conduct the code reading, you'll see obvious places where you can change it and learn what it does.

Configuring this program starts with the variable named `TARGETS`. It's an array of objects that represents list of websites the program will tell PhantomJS to snapshot, at what size, and the filename prefix. This can be as long or as short as you want it to be. Pick your work-in-progress website running on localhost, an inspirational one out on the Internet, or a customer's existing site that you want to redo.

Exercising some code style rules, I've named this variable with all uppercase letters, signifying that it is a constant and ought not to be changed by the program as it runs.

```
var TARGETS = [{
    url: 'http://www.threethumbisland.com',
    width: 1280,
    height: 1280,
```

```
        fileName: '3Thumb'
    }, {
        url: 'http://www.threethumbisland.com',
        width: 1024,
        height: 1280,
        fileName: '3Thumb'
    }, {
        url: 'http://www.threethumbisland.com',
        width: 768,
        height: 1280,
        fileName: '3Thumb'
    }, {
        url: 'http://www.threethumbisland.com',
        width: 320,
        height: 1280,
        fileName: '3Thumb'
    }];
```

This section includes another module from PhantomJS that has to do with a way to run another program from within this one. Engineers use the term "spawn" to represent a program that comes from another. "Process" has to do with a program running on a computer, and "child" refers to the nature of a program coming from another. We might call the original program a parent.

An important variable called numFinish is set to 0. This program counts as it sees child screen shot programs finishing and exiting.

```
var spawn = require('child_process').spawn;
var numFinished = 0;
```

JavaScript has a forEach function attached to arrays. Using it lets us send a little function that's called by every element stored in the array. Several arguments are sent into the function. It's just the way it works.

```
TARGETS.forEach(function shootTarget(target, index, array) {
```

Here we use the PhantomJS spawn library required into our program. It has two parameters: the program to run and an array of command-line arguments sent to it. In this case, the program is PhantomJS and the array of values is the `WebPageScreenShot.JS` program we wrote earlier and all of the elements of the particular target from the overall array of `TARGETS`. Using the `forEach` function on the array guarantees that we can see each and every target object one at a time.

```
var child;

child = spawn('phantomjs', ['WebPageScreenShot.js',
target.width, target.height, target.url,
target.fileName]);
```

Children have a few functions available to them, and using the on function lets us attach callback functions that listen for events. The first event is when data come from `stdout`. As an engineer, I learned years ago that `stdout` is a contraction for "standard out"—text coming out from a command-line utility. We've done that earlier by using the `console.log` function to write text.

Using it in this way grabs output from the child program and displays it from this program as if it were the author. We redirect output to give feedback that reassures our user that things are happening.

```
child.stdout.on('data', function (data) {
    console.log(data);
});
```

When a child program finishes, the next event handler is tickled, and we keep count. When we've seen the same number finish that were started, we tell PhantomJS to clean up after itself, and we exit. It's all done.

```
child.on('exit', function () {
    numFinished += 1;
    if (numFinished === TARGETS.length) {
        phantom.exit(0);
    }
});
});
```

I like this example because it shows how we built a simple tool and then built another tool that uses the first one. Composing programs from smaller ones is a great way to save time and effort. Automation removes the friction of everyday boredom from human beings who think they're good at following directions but in fact are very bad at it. They want to have their opinions heard and get creative as they do things. Often that's the magic of people, but in this case, it's a variable to be optimized away. We'd rather have the computer tirelessly do the repetitive task and let us interpret the reports it provides.

How does it report? Let's take a look at what these automated screens provide and how you might use them.

Use This Power Tool

Now that we have this tool— in fact, several tools—at our disposal, how do we use them? Are they ready? Yes, most assuredly, but don't let that stop you from working on them and improving them over time. Here are several ways you can use them based on what I've experienced. I'm also including ideas I heard from some community friends when I showed this work to them.

INTERNAL DESIGN CRITIQUES

Gather the team around a wall with printouts of your latest and greatest screen shots. Provide a survey of how the website design looks across a breadth of device shapes. Use this focus time to build shared understanding of what's been done. Hand out pads of sticky notes and black markers to everyone, ask for their comments, and stick them on the printouts to move forward with purpose.

WEEKLY DESIGN COMP DELIVERABLES TO CUSTOMERS

When visiting clients for status updates, bring an assortment of printouts of screen shots that show how their upcoming site will look across a series of devices. Choose device sizes that represent their customers. Let them see how their company's content will read on phones, tablets, and laptops. No need for surprises once their site has gone live. Educate them early, and discover incorrect assumptions as soon as possible.

USABILITY TESTING HANDOUTS

Run a usability test to find out how potential customers understand a site. Present a collection of printouts of your site at various sizes and ask a participant if they could figure out how to do a series of useful actions. Will they understand how an off-screen menu operates? Do they see the shopping cart options? Does a screen shrink away key call-to-action buttons that they will miss? Find out these bad user-experience issues as early as possible. Corrections are always cheaper and easier before the site goes live.

Give each test subject their own fresh set of printouts and encourage them to talk through their internal thoughts and mark up the pages. Bring these back to your designers, product owners, and developers to let them see what your test subjects saw. Mistakes are never failures if we choose to learn from them.

HISTORY ALBUM

Imagine keeping an audit trail of these screen shots. Storage space is cheap, after all.

Compare present-day screen shots to past ones. Watch how your website has progressed over time and how your design is evolving.

Presenting a trail of images that shows how a website has changed over time is powerful. Most things will get better over time, so pay attention to the few things that get worse. Now is the time to revert to the old way if it was better. You can more easily make these judgments when everything is side by side.

Admire polish. Show off your history album at the celebration launch party.

BRAG BOOK

It's great to have a physical portfolio to show a perspective client or employer. Sitting down for a meeting in person and showing all your past work is a fantastic way to learn if a new job is a match. Use this tool to generate screen shots of your best work across a sample of typical devices sizes. Let your work speak for your attention to detail, design layout, content strategy, and overall professional level of owning results. Always be ready to demo your best work. Post these to your online portfolio as well.

IMAGEMAGICK

Let's bring in another tool to process data for us. It's called ImageMagick and is used for image processing and manipulation. Saying it's one tool isn't correct because it's a bundle of several tools that serve unique individual purposes. Of course, they all run on the command line. Each of them is interesting because each can be used in a script, or simple program, to automate steps, as computers are so good at doing. What data would I want them to process? Website screen shots that our tools write.

One of the tools in the ImageMagick set is particularly interesting to me. It's called `compare`, and it allows us to give it two images and it will compare them. How? By conducting image processing on them to figure out the differences between them, if any. Its output is a third file that displays any and all differences between your two images. "Fantastic and powerful" is what comes to my mind given a history of screen shots from your website.

ABOUT IMAGE PROCESSING

Image processing works because all pictures stored on the computer are collections of pixels. You know pixels very well by this time in your career. When you're editing an image, you'll see each pixel stacked up in column-and-row format to make up any image.

When you're saving a file out from ImageMagick, you can pick its file type and the compression algorithm it uses. You want to choose this based on the type of image it is. If it's UI or a logo, you should go with a PNG. If it's a photo, you should go with a JPEG. Why? Photos can lose a lot of data and still look fine, while UI elements and logos typically can't. Compression lets the PNG format keep its files smaller than raw ones, but it never throws away pixels while shrinking them—it's lossless compression. Throwing away pixels from a picture might seem unusual to you, but in fact, the JPEG file format has a highly compressed scheme that does— it's lossy compression. Depending on how high you crank up the compression factor, more pixel detail is removed by its algorithm in pursuit of maximum space saving.

Comparing images stored in the JPEG file format is a problem because they will always give false positives. Plenty of pixel drift will happen between any two images, even when they start from the same source, every time they're saved to JPEG. It's the nature of the powerful math behind the compressor that makes the files so small.

For these reasons, I typically prefer the PNG image format.

INSTALLING IMAGEMAGICK

You'll want to install ImageMagick once you've read through this chapter and decided that it's a powerful tool to add to your professional toolbox. Please look to the download page on the creators' official website for instructions on installing ImageMagick:

```
http://www.imagemagick.org/script/binary-releases.php
```

I believe the information you'll read there is clearly written and current. There's no need for this book to duplicate that effort. On that page, you'll find information regarding downloading and installing this tool on both OS X and Windows.

COMPARING TWO IMAGES

The math behind comparing two images consists of reading both image files and stepping through their pixels row by row, column by column. Each RGB (red, green, blue) color is compared to the opposing mate on the other image. Producing accurate results means comparing two images of the same size and color depth (8-bit, 16-bit, 24-bit color).

Computers are perfect for following steps like comparing in this precise manner. Humans say they can compare two images and tell us the difference, but in fact we're not good at it at all. We get bored, we interpret images based on point of view, and we're biased, meaning we'll go hard or take it easy when comparing based on our emotional attachment to the image's contents or creator.

As a computer program compares each pixel color, it will use a low-level mathematical operator called XOR. It's an example of binary logic. Binary is the yes-or-no answer that fundamentally powers a computer to its core. XOR, shorthand for exclusive or, is the perfect tool for comparative image processing. This table shows how it works at the lowest level of a computer's digital brain:

```
0 XOR 0 = false

0 XOR 1 = true

1 XOR 0 = true

1 XOR 1 = false
```

Every image file has pixels, each of those pixels has a red, green, and blue color, and each of those can be broken down into zeroes and ones. When an XOR between two numbers is true or false, it lets the image-processing tool decide how to act. If this binary math doesn't exactly make sense to you, then please trust me on this one, and let's keep moving forward.

VISUAL DIFFERENCING

ImageMagick's compare tool considers two images and writes a third file that annotates distortions between the inputs. Using it is as simple as:

1. From the command line, change directory into the folder in which you have saved the images

2. Enter the command `compare picture1.png picture2.png picture3.png` and wait a few seconds for it to work

3. You'll find a newly created image file called `picture3.png` that compares the two images. Feel free to open it in your favorite viewer and have a look at what it found. You'll see a fuzzy red color every place it found a difference between the two images.

Anna's Spelling Words

Helping you practice for the spelling test. Study hard, good luck, and see you next week!

Friday May 2, 2014
Contractions

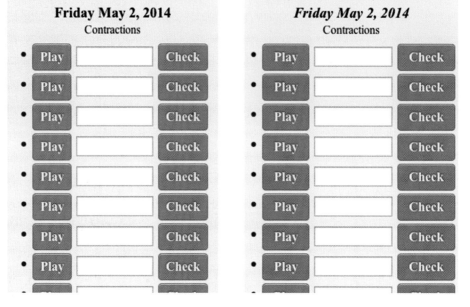

- Play [ ] Check
- Play [ ] Check
- Play [ ] Check
- Play [ ] Check
- Play [ ] Check
- Play [ ] Check
- Play [ ] Check
- Play [ ] Check

Anna's Spelling Words

Helping you practice for the spelling test. Study hard, good luck, and see you next week!

Friday May 2, 2014
Contractions

- Play [ ] Check
- Play [ ] Check
- Play [ ] Check
- Play [ ] Check
- Play [ ] Check
- Play [ ] Check
- Play [ ] Check
- Play [ ] Check

Anna's Spelling Words

Helping you practice for the spelling test. Study hard, good luck, and see you next week!

Friday May 2, 2014
Contractions

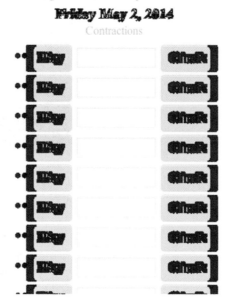

In the example's results, you'll see two apparently similar screen shots of a website I'm running on my localhost. Ask a human what the differences are and they might say they see none, while others will notice something obvious. Our tireless computer shows exactly the differences based on various CSS tweaks I made—for example, minor tweaks to padding, font color, and an italics style.

I demoed this tool at a conference once. After the session, an audience member told me that their website has a lot of reddish colors, the same color ImageMagick defaults to when showing the differences between two images. He guessed it would be hard to recognize what was supposed to be there and what wasn't. At the time, I didn't know if the compare tool would write out a comparison image showing differences in another color. But it can! I've looked up the answer, and you can use the argument `highlight-color`.

USE THIS POWER TOOL

Another powerful tool is available to you with this comparing utility. How can you use it? Engineers are seemingly always creating logic bugs. Every change we make gives us another chance to make a human error, and we look to test for newly introduced glitches and bugs. Quality-assurance testers call those regressions. It suggests something has gone backward in its capability.

Can we make visual bugs? Absolutely, and anytime we significantly change the CSS to update a design, there's a chance of doing so. CSS is a programming language, and like any, it sets us up for making errors while we're building software with it. If we're taking screen shots regularly with `MultiShot.JS` and `WebPageScreenShot.JS`, we have an audit trail. Comparing daily changes against well-known past successes, we can casually find out if there are visual differences. Then we can decide if those reports are good or bad. Expected changes are fine, but surprises must be validated.

Alternatives for Image Diffing

If you have screen shots created with PhantomJS but you don't want to use ImageMagick to create the comparison image, there are GUI tools to help with that:

- Kaleidoscope is a file-comparison application available for purchase on OS X. The product website describes how you can use it for spotting the differences between two text files, such as source code, but it's also visual. Instead of using the ImageMagick command-line tool, you could replace it with Kaleidoscope.

- Beyond Compare is another commercial app with image file comparison. It's available for MS Windows, and you could use it instead of ImageMagick. It shows the visual differences between two images.

Alternatives for PhantomJS

SlimerJS is a headless browser that runs on the command line and uses JavaScript for extra scripting control. The Gecko engine performs all rendering, and that's the same one that powers Firefox. Gecko is very similar to PhantomJS, which uses WebKit. It could be considered a replacement for PhantomJS.

EXTENDING PHANTOMJS

CasperJS is a library that makes it easier to use PhantomJS by providing a helpful high-level interface. Writing scripts to automate everything you want to do with a headless browser might be simpler with CasperJS.

Commandeering the Command Line

Engineers' tools often seem unfriendly and hard to understand—much like the people who create them. Joking aside, I hope you've seen here how many useful tools exist in the world. It's well worth your time to experiment with them, learn them well, and gain confidence in this environment. You'll see that routine tasks are accomplished quickly, especially when automation is brought into the mix. The JavaScript programs you wrote controlling PhantomJS are solid examples of how you can automatically generate website screen shots for documentation, team critiques, and client delivery.

Perhaps I'm comfortable with the command line because I grew up with it. My computing career started decades ago, when there weren't any graphical user interfaces. It was absolutely a case of do or die for me. Today, we have a choice, but history influences our present selections. We can use these command-line tools manually, on a timer, or automated by build tools that detect source-code changes submitted to revision control systems.

Being lazy should be a point of pride. We invest a little time early on, creating automation, it pays off big over time. Time saved comes as a result of the virtual software robots we make do our bidding without our direct intervention or constant scrutiny.

CHAPTER 12

Looking Around the Toolbox

Hammering Responsive Web Design Into Shape

Choosing to pick up this book and go through it at whatever speed you did separates you from your competition. That drive to pursue quality makes you remarkable. This book is useless to someone who doesn't have the desire to learn. It's loaded with strategies and tactics, but only those with a passion for domain mastery will find ways to apply them for great use. Propel yourself forward with curiosity as you respond to the constant changes technology makes in the world. Always have the goal of creating wonderful things.

No matter where you are in your career, this book was created to help you stretch out in amazing ways. The main focus of this book was to help you hammer responsive web designs into shape by providing you a toolbox and the understanding of when and what to reach for. More than that, I want to show you how to build up and maintain your toolbox and expertise so that you can thrive into the future. To be successful, you need to hustle to keep up with the current trends, take time to learn new skills, and outwork the competition.

HOW TO CONNECT WITH ME

Let me add value to you through our further conversation. Follow me on Twitter and allow me to continue updating you with future discoveries on industry best practice. Please send me feedback regarding this book and what you've found most useful about it. Definitely reach out to me with helpful suggestions on how I can improve it. Have requests for richer details on anything? Ping me on whatever you found in the book that you want to know more about. My Twitter handle is `@KenTabor`, and I invite you to connect with me there. You can also find me on LinkedIn just as easily.

Even as this book draws to a conclusion I'm going to keep writing. There's always something new to share with you. Look for my continued exploration of tools, user experience, programming, and leadership at the website dedicated to this book.

```
www.HammeringResponsiveWebDesign.com
```

Keep an eye on this website, because I'm updating it with fresh sample code and links to useful resources I find on the Internet. I'm totally driven to learn and solve interesting problems, and promise to report the results back to you. When I find several people are asking the same question I'll take it as a clue to roll up a useful answer on the book's website.

OTHER RESOURCES AVAILABLE TO YOU

Reading this book and taking on the exercise of learning the lessons contained within it is a fantastic step in your continuing education. Pick up these tools over time and break them in, making them fit comfortably in your confident hand. Select them and strike challenges. Your creative toolbox is now enhanced with powerful additions. You've seen reasons to use them and guidance on when they aren't as helpful.

Some have advanced applications that this book hasn't approached. Some of the resources listed will help you learn further uses. When you're ready to know more, keep an eye on these sites, looking for improvements.

Newsletters are carefully curated guides made by editors with a particular outlook. I appreciate these tireless individuals sifting through the vast amounts of content published daily on blogs, corporate newsrooms, Twitter channels, and formal journals. I'll gladly subscribe to a newsletter matching my point of view. I prefer ones published weekly. It's a perfect schedule for me to seek out new stuff.

```
Web Tools Weekly - http://webtoolsweekly.com/
Web Design Weekly - http://web-design-weekly.com/
Software Lead Weekly - http://softwareleadweekly.com/
Mobile Web Weekly - http://mobilewebweekly.co/
UX Design Weekly - http://uxdesignweekly.com/
JavaScript Weekly - http://javascriptweekly.com/
```

Community-based websites organizing members toward solving problems for each other are fantastic resources when CSS, HTML, and JavaScript get tricky. Most days, I think I couldn't do my job if the Internet connection dropped for more than a few hours. Check out these sites for help when you're getting confused on how to approach a problem.

```
Stack Overflow - http://stackoverflow.com/
CSS-Tricks - http://css-tricks.com/
```

```
Web Designer Depot - http://www.webdesignerdepot.com/
A List Apart - http://alistapart.com/
Smashing Magazine - http://www.smashingmagazine.com/
Web Resources Depot - http://www.webresourcesdepot.com/
Code Pen - http://codepen.io/
DailyJS - http://dailyjs.com/
Tuts+ - http://code.tutsplus.com/
```

Think of visiting these sites when you don't have questions. Browse around and volunteer an answer or insight when you see someone looking for help. Don't think that you lack credibility and shouldn't hit the reply button. Take the time to add your voice to the chorus. If all you have is a small insight, add it, because even a tiny boost will lead the group toward a complete answer.

Another way of learning is letting the open-source community update you. Who are the authors of your favorite frameworks, libraries, and plugins? Look up who started them and who are the most active maintainers today, and follow them on Twitter. Most of them can be found there. You'll see they're actively sending out public messages reviewing tools they've discovered and update notices to their own work. Here are some to get you started.

```
Chrome Developers - @ChromiumDev
IE Dev Chat - @IEDevChat
Paul Irish - @paul_irish
Ariya Hidayat (PhantomJS) - @AriyaHidayat
Adobe Web Platform - @adobeweb
Ben Alman (Grunt) - @cowboy
Hampton Catlin (Sass) - @hcatlin
Adam Sontag (jQuery) - @ajpiano
Timothy Fontaine (NodeJS) - @tjfontaine
```

As you follow and get to know some creators, see who they're following. They can lead you to know more voices contributing to your knowledge.

Benefits of a Loaded Toolbox

MASTER THESE TOOLS

This book mapped out a journey that we've taken together. Dozens of tools were uncovered throughout it. Many of them will be useful and valuable discoveries, improving your creative work. What should you do with them now? Become a complete master of them. Apply them to your jobs and push them to their limits. All of these tools are software, they're virtual and exist only inside the computer, but so too they are present in our minds. Envisioning how and when to use these tools programs us to a certain extent. If that's true, then mastering your tools means mastering yourself. Practicing this leads to true strength beyond any particular job, client, team, or season of life. Instinctively recognizing a problem's pattern and understanding what type of tool to reach for is the modern-day muscle memory of a knowledge worker.

Teaching is a fantastic way to increase mastery of craft. Select any tool or technique that you're passionate about and consider how you can share your knowledge of it. Write an article on a blog site, host a lunch-and-learn at work, present at a local professional meet-up, or speak at a conference. I find the total despair of failing hard in front of a group of people focuses me like no other motivator to produce results. It focuses me to learn my subject so well that I can stand up in front of an audience and confidently tell them everything I know. Once you become confident, bestow your knowledge on your community.

Don't let imposter syndrome stop you from doing service like this. I've found that any competent person feels they don't know enough about a specific subject. They'll imagine that they're not qualified enough to talk about it. That's the dumbest thing a smart person believes. Imagining that everyone else knows more on a subject than you do is so disabling. Don't fall for it. Have strength to volunteer your time delivering valuable insights to an audience. It's worth it, and you'll reap the positive rewards of serving others. I've never had the author of a tool in any of my talks. I've never had someone so experienced using a tool that they asked an impossible question, revealing an embarrassing gap in my understanding. They don't show up to my talks. You know who shows up? People who want to learn. Go meet them and do a good job teaching them! You'll never feel more pride than having an audience member say thank you after a talk. You'll never be more grateful than when you connect with an audience member and learn something from them.

COMBINE THESE TOOLS

Physical tools are generally built to solve one problem well and a second problem passably. For example, a screwdriver is great for turning a screw into a wall but hardly good at smashing a nail halfway. Hammers are fantastic for driving a nail into the wall but only adequate as pry bars. Software tools are virtually real and simply exist as zeroes and ones inside the computer's memory. That means they can be shaped and extended to our needs. Take advantage of that opportunity, because their creators often intend it to happen.

Explore ways of connecting tools, making their results go farther than they ever could solo. Solve more interesting problems, creating your own tool chain. Automation goes a long way toward helping you develop custom tools that run in order—especially command-line tools because they're made for that sort of job. Automating routine tasks by making the computer do them is a big win for you because it saves time and the tedium of repetition. Repeating tasks makes human beings bored, but it's something computers excel at.

Every modern operating system has built in ways of writing brief shell scripts that simulates the commands you would run by hand. Examples are changing directories, creating files, running utilities, executing tools, and issuing alerts on the results. These could be shell scripts, batch files, or another type depending on what your computer runs.

Cross-platform scripting tools exist. This is especially interesting when you're in a large enterprise with lots of people and varied systems. For example, your engineering team might be running Windows, your design team OS X, and your operations team Linux. Scripting helpful tool chain processes in a language such as NodeJS, Ruby, or Python becomes interesting when we think of this mixed environment. Languages like these are higher level and offer you helpful support because they're feature rich and have extensive libraries.

If writing automation scripts in a computer language or operating system shell feels intimidating or goes beyond your time limit, then check out some of the task runners that have popped up in the open-source community. They can offer a time-saving boost when you want to automate tasks. A few examples of these that have formed helpful communities are:

```
Grunt  -  http://gruntjs.com/
Yeoman  -  http://yeoman.io/
Chef  -  http://chef.io/
Gulp  -  http://gulpjs.com/
Bower  -  http://bower.io/
Jenkins  -  http://jenkins-ci.org/
```

REPLACE THESE TOOLS

Technology has a shelf date—it expires. Not as horribly as a jug of milk does, but you know when tech just isn't as tasty as it used to be. Real-world tools make it obvious when they need replacing. As soon as they chip, crack, and curl, we see it's time to head down to the neighborhood hardware store and buy a new one. Software tools are less clear. We have a look at the files they turn out or how slowly they run or if they're incompatible with the most valuable of our other tools.

You've seen that tools emerge from the creative minds of the open-source community with great frequency. It can be confusing knowing which ones to incorporate into your daily creative workflow. It's confusing even knowing which ones to download and evaluate. From my perspective, changing tools is an effort, and I reserve specific time for looking into them. Instinct tells me when I've had a tool long enough that it might need replacement with the fresher alternative. I scan the community chatter on Twitter and look at conference presentations published online. When something is referred enough, I give it a look.

Generally I'll take time to play with a new software tool at home on a hobby project. Then I bring it in to work, giving the team a demo. I'm seeing if my internal customers are intrigued enough to encourage further work with it or if anyone already knows a show-stopping fact about it—for example, it's too expensive, intrusive, or incompatible. If I already like the tool enough I might engage in a little sales effort to convert my team, but I always listen first to understand their perspective.

Ultimately your deciding factors for picking up a new tool might be informed by asking a few simple questions:

- Does it solve a problem that you have?
- Has it attracted a dedicated and helpful community?
- Can it swap out relatively easily with a similar tool in your creative workflow?
- Will you and your team have time to try it for a week?

Giving a new tool a week is one of the most important things. Letting it have a proper chance to settle into your daily routine is how you'll have the best idea of its value. Then you can decide if it's a successful addition and if it will become a part of your creative toolbox.

When you decide the time is right to take on a new tool, then do so decisively. Don't delay. Focus up the team to get behind the change and embrace it entirely. There's rarely a good time to make a change, so you might as well get it done now and never look back. Avoid incurring so-called technical debt by avoiding making the tough decisions. The last complication you want is some people on a new tool and others on a legacy one. Ideally, everyone on the team will rapidly come up to speed and train one another on what they learn.

Staring Out the Window

Where do ideas come from? I think they mostly come from staring out the window. Sometimes they come from reading Twitter, but mostly it's a matter of daydreaming. Once an idea pops into your head, give it time. Talking about it immediately might be a mistake. No one wants to hear "I don't get it" after sharing a new idea with somebody. In truth, fresh ideas need time for polishing and thoughtful consideration of how they help. Any creative idea must transform from novel into valuable.

Check out the new tools coming from the open-source community. Challenge the personal bias that you already know how to get from point A to point B. Mindfully open yourself up to new ways of doing things to pop off the well-worn route in order to find new pathways. They can lead to whatever fashion of success you need. Work with your team to brainstorm new ideas using the improvisational comedy technique of "yes and. . ." Practice accepting and escalating ideas together until you've collectively discovered new ways of working.

Sometimes the office simply doesn't provide the purely creative environment you need to learn new tech. Don't let that hold you back from discovery. Personal hobby projects are fantastic experiments in which you can pull in new technology and apply it in any way you see fit. Hobby projects don't have budgets or time limits or market pressures. Use them to take a test drive of some library or framework that you want to understand in real-world situations. If it doesn't seem useful, no worries—just abandon it. No need to follow through on a hobby project when it shows no promise. Intriguing results are worth a show and tell with your teammates the next day. Run it through its paces and let everyone decide whether it's fit for your purpose.

Have a Coffee, and Let's Do Something Awesome Today

I relish drinking coffee. Yes, it was an acquired taste, and I didn't totally get it the first few times I ordered it. Now there's something about coffee that makes me think sharper, dream deeper, and take more positive action throughout the day. It's something that I look forward to and keep near in my heart. Many of the concepts in this book may form questions and fill you with doubt at first. It's a perfectly valid reaction, and please consider each for a while. Fully expect that many of these will become acquired tastes, and you'll happily surprise yourself when they grow into daily use.

When you fully master the tools shown in this book, don't stop there. Feeling expertise is a trap. Be innocent like a child and continue wondering about the world. Mindfully push forward and lean into the edges of what you understand. Combine the tools in unique ways as only software can do in the virtual reality of computers. Search out their communities and find new places they lead you. Don't be shy telling people about what you've done. Show your teammates and local community what you're doing and contribute a bit of value in their lives. Sharing what you know with others will make you feel good, and it might spark a connection with a new collaborator.

Just as there are seemingly limitless ways for me to enjoy coffee, I take pleasure in finding new tools to better build websites. Let's enjoy what we have now, but promise to continue discovering more together. I'll update you through the book's website, `www. HammeringResponsiveWebDesign.com`, and I invite you to chat back to me through Twitter `@KenTabor`.

Let's do something awesome today!

Anna's Section

As a father to a daughter, I've found that writing this book is an incredible teachable moment. Anna has grown up with a house full of books, and opening her eyes to the possibility of creating one is great fun for me. I hope it inspires her to take on future challenges.

One Tuesday morning, as I woke up Anna for the day, I told her that I had good news. After getting her to bed the previous night, I had written 500 words and finished off Chapter 9. She replied that that was good work, but I still had four chapters to go. She knew very well that I had skipped Chapter 2 because I didn't have inspiration to start it. Anna warned that this left a hole in my book and wondered how could I know where the story would go.

I love the way she thinks and assured her it wasn't a problem because it's not that kind of book. It's to teach rather than tell a story. My plan was to complete more of the book and then go back to Chapter 2. That way I could set up common ideas and themes once I discovered them. At that point, Anna jumped out of bed. She said she'd help me write some of Chapter 2 while I made breakfast. I went to the kitchen to get started while she grabbed a pencil and paper and started working in the living room.

Catching a quick peek at my daughter, I saw her a study of concentration as she labored over her work. She's always been a creative person, but with her being age 7, I had no idea exactly what she'd come up with. We had to get the day started, but I was willing to wait while she finished. I've always encouraged her to have her own ideas and follow through whatever she starts.

Anna walked up to me with her paper in hand, ready to hear my response. Of course I gave her my full attention. Looking straight into her earnest face, I listened as she read her report. When you see it on the next page, you can easily guess how proud I was of her. After Anna read her page, all I needed to do was give her a big hug and a smile. I could tell she was pleased with her writing and was ready for us to chow down on some tasty breakfast.

As a father and programmer, it's a privilege that I can share my passion for writing code with my daughter. We've finished many projects in the past and this book most recently. I can't wait to see what our future holds!

Eye Pad's are flat but a phone is ismal and flatt but a cumpeewtr is a holl difrent thing. It is shaped difrent it is like two eye pads poosht to geth to make one cumpeewtr. a cumpeewtr has one skreen and unuthrskreen but in sted of a smooth srfis it as bottons with Pickchrs.

by: Anna Tabor

Index